Smart Girls Don't

and Guys Don't Either

Dr. Kevin Leman

Regal Books
A Division of GL Publications
Ventura, CA U.S.A.

The foreign language publishing of all Regal books is under the direction of GLINT. GLINT provides financial and technical help for the adaptation, translation and publishing of books for millions of people worldwide. For information regarding translation contact: GLINT, P.O. Box 6688, Ventura, California 93006.

Published by Regal Books
A Division of GL Publications
Ventura, California 93006
Printed in U.S.A.

Library of Congress Cataloging in Publication Data
Leman, Kevin
    Smart girls don't, and guys don't either.

    Includes bibliographical references.
        1. Youth—Sexual behavior.   2. Adolescent psychology.
3. Parenting.   4. Dating (Social customs)   I. Title.
HQ796.L366 1982   305.2'35   82-7686
ISBN 0-8307-0824-3   AACR2

DEDICATION

This book is affectionately dedicated to my Dad and Mom, John and May Leman, who persistently encouraged me, throughout my difficult adolescent years. More importantly, they had the courage to tell me what was right and wrong, and the wisdom to allow me to make the choice.

ACKNOWLEDGEMENTS

Thank you to Richard Kuykendall for his invaluable assistance in the research for this book.

Thank you to Carol Lacy for her encouragement, support and tireless contributions to the manuscript.

And thank *you* for buying this book. Without people like you there wouldn't be any successful books or authors.

Contents

Introduction: Entering a Teenager's Private World

Adolescence. What is it? It's the most frightening, bewildering, exciting, chaotic time most people will ever go through. And it happens to a kid at a time when he is the most vulnerable; so vulnerable that even one little thing—"little" to his parents—can disrupt his life and leave a permanent scar.

The parents of an adolescent sometimes think he is trying to cram a whole lifetime in just six months. He wants to test and try and taste just about everything that comes along. And nothing is normal size; everything is exaggerated. A simple pimple can become Mount St. Helens in a teenager's life.

We're so saturated with stories about the turmoils of teenagers that we have come to believe that the problems which adolescents face have been around since the beginning of time. But this isn't true. According to Ronald L. Koteskey in the article "Growing Up Too Late Too Soon," adolescence is a phenomenon since only the last century. Adolescence did not and still does not exist in preliterate, agrarian societies. Adolescence occurs only in

industrial societies where the age of economic independence and marriage is delayed past puberty.[1]

Adolescence is a creation of our culture and not of
God; therefore, the Bible does not give specific instruction on the subject of adolescence. How, then, are we as
parents supposed to know how to help our teenagers
through this critical period of their lives?

We put just about all our time, energy, sweat, and
labor of love into raising our children only to realize,
about midway through their teen years, that everything
we've done is often offset by the influence of complete
strangers—our children's peers. We discover that our kids
are paying more attention to their friends than they are to
what we say. But one thing is sure—they do pay attention
to what we *do*!

I was working, in my private counseling practice, with
a mom and her 16-year-old son. We were making pretty
good progress with the 16-year-old until the day he got
stopped by a police officer and was found with an open
bottle of Ripple wine in the automobile. The mother
reacted with such rage that she was still visibly upset six
days after the incident when they came to see me.

As we were talking in the office with her son, her son
asked her a very direct question. "Didn't you ever have
something to drink and drive at the same time?"

Mom shouted, "Of course I didn't," and I about fell
off my chair. This woman was an alcoholic. Surely she
drove while drinking at some point in her life.

After her son left the room I turned to her in disbelief
and asked, "Do you mean to say that you never operated
a car when you were drinking or drunk?"

She answered, "Of course I have. I've driven under
the influence several times. But I certainly didn't want
him to know that." I hadn't been fooled by her protesta-
tions, and neither had her son. What a tragic mistake this

mom had made. Perhaps if she had had the courage to share her mistakes, her son could have reaped the benefit of her experiences and wouldn't have had to go through them himself.

If we're going to have any kind of communication with our teenagers we must be willing to share our real selves with them, not just the ideal selves we'd like them to think we are. Kids pay very little attention to parental words. They pay particular attention to parental actions. If we parents are going to enter the private world of teenagers, we must be brave enough to be open and to share some of the realities and complexities of our own lives. Sometimes it's difficult to go back to our adolescent years and rekindle the thoughts and feelings we had as teenagers. In fact many of us who are successful at rekindling memories of our teenage years react by getting uptight at our own teenagers for those very reasons. We fear that our children are going to make the same kind of mistakes we made during adolescence.

We tend to forget that we're all crummy and not perfect; each of us makes mistakes. Yet in spite of that, most of us have people who are close to us and love us, warts and all. Our kids already know that we are imperfect by nature in spite of the smoke screen we throw out, and we miss great opportunities when we don't share our flaws openly with them for fear they will think less of us. We will be much more approachable and, therefore, more able to help our kids if we can share the realities of our own lives and experiences with them. I know it isn't always easy to be honest about our own weaknesses.

I am often put on the spot as a counselor because people tend to think I have the answers to all of life's problems. I was doing a network television show once and had a call from a viewer who asked a very complicated question about abortion. The woman had three children, was 20 years of age, was being pulled both ways by her mom and her husband, and wanted to know what to do about her unwanted pregnancy. Well, those kinds of questions shouldn't be answered in 20 seconds or less. I backed off by simply saying that I felt I couldn't answer that kind of question in the short time provided. I should have been honest and said, "I don't know what you should do. I need more information from you before I can help you decide."

The host of the show looked at me as if to say, "You mean to say that we flew you 3,000 miles and you don't have an answer for the lady?" Then he went on to answer the question for the young woman.

Many of us have great expectations put upon us. I've found throughout my seminars that when I am brave enough to dig down and share myself with others, they in turn open up and share their hearts as well. That's a good situation where each of us can learn and grow if we'll approach each other with a spirit of acceptance and sincerity.

I must admit that as a psychologist and author of books on parenthood and marriage I am sensitive to how people view me and my family. I feel that everyone thinks my children and my marriage ought to be perfect. But to my children I'm just Daddy. I'm not a psychologist or Dr. Leman. I'm just Daddy. (And sometimes the Big Bad Wolf. I must admit I play the role of the Big Bad Wolf as well as anyone.) I don't have all the answers, but in this book we'll talk about many things—hard subjects such as understanding your teenagers, conformity to peers, dating and sex, love, communication, booze and drugs—and maybe together we can find some answers to a few of your adolescent's problems.

If I ever get to the place where I begin to believe about myself what other people believe about me, my family can bring me back to reality. My wife Sande is really the sounding board in my life. She's my closest friend. She's everything I would ever want in a wife. She keeps me humble and very honest. For example, I was gone on a speaking engagement one weekend and came home to see the water trickling down the street from our garden hose. One thing that really gets me mad is when my children play with the hose in the front of the house and let the water run. Now, when I'm gone for three days from my wife and kids I really miss them. But this time my first words as I walked into the house were, "Who the heck left the water running in the front of the house?"

My wife yelled from the kitchen, "Oh, he's home, the family counselor."

Well, all of us have a way of putting ourselves on pedestals inferring that we are above the problems other people have. My observation, as I look at the American family today, is that all families have problems of one kind or another. And every person in the family has imperfections and shortcomings and is, in the true sense, crummy and imperfect. When we can all admit this, then and only then can we begin to make progress in ministering to one another.

In order to get our kids through these turbulent, wild years called *adolescence* we as parents must be willing to take the first step to enter into their private world. In order for us to do that we must first establish a spirit of cooperation and of equality, equality meaning that we're not going to deal with them as superiors, but we *are* going to approach them as parents placed, by God, in authority over them. Equality means to begin to open up and share experiences with our children in such a way that maybe our experiences will, in the long run, be helpful to our kids.

Chapter 1

Is There an Adolescent in the House?

I f you were to ask most parents of teenagers what an adolescent is, they would probably not be too kind in their description. Many a parent has marveled at the great change his or her child undergoes as he becomes an adolescent. All of a sudden this kid who never got within six feet of a washrag his whole life now stands before a mirror scrubbing his face until it glistens; he shampoos and blow-dries his hair at least once a day and sometimes more, seeking perfection. The adolescent daughter takes a bath and leaves the water running continuously—with the stopper still in—so the "schmootz" floating on the water runs out through the overflow drain instead of sticking to her body.

This excessive concern with their physical appearance is tremendously burdensome for many teenagers because it's during their adolescent years that they encounter all kinds of physical problems: skin blemishes, lack of coordination, tongue-tiedness, and a disturbing emerging sexual awareness. Research substantiates the fact that sex drive is probably the greatest during those late teenage years—16-18.

All of these seemingly negative factors contribute to our adolescent's self-esteem. It's critical that we as parents understand that the poorer a teenager's self-esteem is, the greater will be the impact others have on his value system. They become more susceptible and vulnerable to the thoughts, wishes and desires of others, especially those of their peers.

Adolescents Want to Be Perfect

Can you imagine a big zit on Marie Osmond's face? Or John Travolta falling over a crack in the sidewalk?

It's no wonder adolescents don't have good feelings about themselves. Look at the models our world portrays to them—John Travolta, Brooke Shields, Donny and Marie Osmond . . . with these examples is it any wonder that adolescents are critical of themselves and others? Teenagers are great flaw-pickers.

If an adolescent happens to be physically different— even in the least way—watch out. Things are going to get a little rough real quickly. And about the first sign that a kid is different is in the nickname other kids put on him.

Thinking about my own teenage years I remember some of the names we gave kids in my peer group— Moonhead, Jughead, Bellhead and Craterhead. I was Craterhead. I happen to have two chickenpox scars on my forehead and one of my "friends" thought that was sort of funny. One evening he branded me "Craterhead." I guess it bothered me enough so that I still remember it. But some in our peer group couldn't handle what they considered derogatory comments, or labels on their appearance.

Adolescents are sensitive about their own differences, but they are critical and sometimes cruel to their peers who are different. I must admit that I was involved in giving the "girl with the flattest chest in the eighth grade" a pair of falsies for her thirteenth birthday. I flinch when I remember the young lady opening that gift at her party in front of all us kids. Of course, most of the guys were gathered together in one corner laughing and screaming and having a great time at this 13-year-old's expense. I remember the many times we used to choose ball teams, and as we "chose up" our teams, more often than not the same kid in our neighborhood was the last one to be picked. I'm surprised he came around as much as he did. After everyone else was chosen, it always got down to, "And you can have Harold." After all, he did bring the ball and bat which entitled him to play right field and bat ninth in our line-up.

How do you suppose teenagers get so sensitive to this whole area of being perfect? For one thing, they're bombarded daily with perfect models proclaiming the virtues of various products—from skin cleansers to soda pop—on the boob tube. Not only that, but those of us who claim to be part of the adult society enforce perfectionism in our own children, particularly in our firstborn children. Why do we think *our* kids have to be best at everything?

In addition to this aspect, our whole perfectionistic society isn't very tolerant of mistakes. Even teachers, who have been trained to be sensitive to children, have the audacity to write at the top of the paper "-3." What's wrong with "+47" at the top of a 50-word spelling test? You see, we've become a society of flaw-pickers.

Have you ever had the experience of sitting in church, listening to a youngster play the flute or clarinet during the offertory, when suddenly the child hits a note that's never been recorded in all of musical history? What kind of feelings went through you when you heard that child make a mistake? Did your heart pound? Did you get very uncomfortable and clammy with embarrassment for the performer? And it wasn't even your kid! As a society we've become too good at thinking in terms of perfection and reinforcing perfectionistic notions in our children's minds.

Adolescents Feel Inferior

James Dobson said it best in his book *Preparing for Adolescence.* He refers to the "canyon of inferiority."[2] If there's one thing that characterizes adolescents, it's that feeling of inferiority; that awkward feeling that says, Nobody else in the world is as ugly as I, as clumsy as I, has as many pimples as I, etc. Of course it doesn't help his adolescent ego when the 14-year-old male answers the phone and the person on the other end of the line says, "Hello, young lady, is your mother home?"

Probably the most common statement parents make about their teenager or young adolescent is that they just don't understand what has happened to their sweet child. Just yesterday little Snooky was so sweet and coopera-tive and loving. But now she's irritable, cantankerous, seeming schizophrenic, volatile and unpredictable.

I believe that self-esteem is probably at an all-time low during the adolescent period. When everything seems to be going wrong, when things seem to be piling up emo-tionally, many teenagers choose to strike out. And who do they strike out at? Those who are the closest—moms, dads, brothers, sisters. Their thinking might be along the line of, "OK, life is being unfair to me so I have a right to strike out."

Why do most kids see themselves as being worth very little during their adolescent period? Prior to adolescence these kids were very well adjusted, happy, good-natured and helpful. But seemingly overnight they turn into something ugly, resentful, moody and even disrespectful.

Many of these feelings, of course, are caused by the

teenager's physical changes. But a great deal of the frustration teenagers suffer is caused by us, their parents. Most parents today, I feel, have done a beautiful job of snowplowing the roads for their children. Christian parents are especially bad about this. We take Proverbs 22:6, *KJV*, "Train up a child in the way he should go and, when he is old, he will not depart from it" to mean that *we* should choose the way he should go—in everything. Donald Gerig, in his book *Leadership in Crisis*, says that parents put the emphasis in the wrong place. It should be on the word "he." "That means that the thrust of this verse is to encourage parents to assist their children in pursuing that direction in life for which they are particularly suited. The verse, then, really says more about vocational choices than it does spiritual choices. Granted, it assumes a spiritual base in which we want God's will, but it then builds on that base by insisting that a focus on God's direction is imperative to a meaningful life." [3]

We as Christian parents think we know what's best for our children, and because we know what's best for them, we haven't given them enough decision-making opportunities. Many times during seminars around the country someone will stop me in midspeech and say, essentially, "Hold on! Now wait a minute. You've gone far enough. I think my wife and I know what's best for our children. And in our home we have rules and regulations and everyone must follow those rules and regulations regardless of how they feel."

After I've given the gentleman the opportunity to speak his mind I usually respond, "Fine. Now who's going to make your child's decision to accept Christ as Lord of his life?" No parents can make that decision for their children. It's the same thing in many other areas of their lives: children and adolescents must be given plenty of opportunities to decide for themselves—of course, with early parental guidance.

Ginny, age 17, was a beautiful young lady. Her blonde hair and blue eyes were accompanied by a beautiful figure and a neat, outgoing personality. To top it off, she was a cheerleader and student body officer. Everybody liked Ginny. Ginny was a Christian. By her own admission she was the only virgin on her high school cheerleading team. Yet she never lacked for male attention.

She was really blessed with a neat relationship with her mom. She could talk with her mother about everything. Frequently after a Friday or Saturday evening date, Ginny and Mom would stay up until after 2:00 A.M. talking about everything from that evening's date to some of the more debatable issues of our society.

One Friday afternoon Ginny came home and told her mother that she wanted to go to a party, a party "everybody" was going to. It was the biggest party of the school year. Ginny asked her mother to drop her off at the party. Because of their open relationship, Ginny told her mom that she was a little concerned because there would probably be some smoking and drinking, and probably pot smoking as well. But it was a party that Ginny wanted very much to attend.

It would have been so easy for Ginny's mom to say, "You're not going to any party, young lady, where there's pot smoking, drinking and such going on. You're going to stay home." But she didn't. She did a very brave thing. She told Ginny that it was her decision, and if she wanted to go Mom would be happy to drop her off. In spite of her many reservations, Ginny still wanted to go. The pluses outweighed the minuses.

Mom dropped her off at the party and, as she did, she said, "Ginny, I'm going to be down the street about half a block. I'm going to wait there for 15 minutes. If things are not what you think they should be, feel free to come on out and I'll give you a ride home."

Well, you guessed it. Ten minutes later Ginny was in the car. "Mom, I couldn't handle it. No way! It was a zoo. There were a lot of older people there, kids from other schools and university students as well. I want to go home."

I often think of Ginny's mom—what a brave woman! She knew what was best for her daughter. It would have been very easy to just say no. But she gave her daughter the right to make the decision about the party. One of the reasons why Ginny's mom could give her that decision-making opportunity was because she had brought her up in a home where from the very beginning Ginny was given choices. So although this was a more sophisticated choice than she had ever made before, she had plenty of practice as a youngster in making decisions.

Being Like Everybody Else Is Important

I'm reminded of the 16-year-old who was in a department store. After selecting a shirt, paying for it and getting it wrapped, he asked the clerk, "Excuse me, if my parents like this shirt, can I return it?"

Teenagers seem to go out of their way to be "in"—but "in" according to their peers' standards. In the early sixties if you were "in" your shirts were button-down shirts. Everything was button-down. One of my cousins watched his father leaving the house dressed in what we referred to as a "fly-away shirt," a shirt without button-down collars. The 15-year-old asked his father, "Are you going out of the house like that?"

What's interesting is that peer pressure seems to be highly evident in early adolescence as well as late adolescence. I worked for 14 years on the University of Arizona campus as Assistant Dean of Students in charge of code of conduct and discipline. I had a ball at registration time! Watching new students come into a university is an experience every parent ought to have. The first few days a freshman student can be spotted a mile away on campus. They're the ones wandering around in a stupor, looking up at the tall buildings, bumping into palm trees, asking stupid questions like, "Excuse me, but could you tell me where the TBA building is?" "TBA" means "to be announced" and it's found in the schedule of classes. It's a very embarrassing question for a college freshman to ask.

But after a couple of weeks even those of us who claim to be experts in the area of students on campus find it very difficult to identify a freshman from the rest of the students. Why? Because freshman read what's expected of them by way of the peer group and blend in. Their dress, demeanor, language, even the way they walk is dictated by the peer group.

In Arizona we enjoy great weather. In December and January it's very common to have 75- and 80-degree days. So our mall is a very popular place for students to gather. I've often thought how much mental effort it must take for a young man or woman to look absolutely cool and detached from all of life as they lay on the mall catching a few rays.

Peer pressure is alive and well even on a college campus where students are quick to point out how individualistic and free of family restraints they are.

Adolescents Are Sexually Aware

Sexual awareness and activity is a very natural part of adolescence. Most adolescents are woefully ill-prepared to deal with and comprehend many changes that are occurring in their bodies. Many children are taught that sex is essentially bad, so they become confused when they experience, at adolescence, the first pleasurable feelings of sex. This may come as a result of self-stimulation or perhaps through fantasizing.

Ronald L. Koteskey, in the article, "Growing Up Too Late Too Soon," points out that parents must recognize the frustrations today's teenagers have. He says that during this "period of celibacy" parents need to recognize that (1) young people face sexual frustration not faced by people a century or more ago; (2) adolescence is a creation of culture, not of God; (3) the Bible does not give direct instruction on this subject; (4) orgasms while asleep and masturbation are likely to occur before marriage.[4]

That brings up another big thing that kids say "everybody's doing." I found that there are two words the Christian community really can't handle very well. The first one is *sex*, and the other is *masturbation*. When either of these words is brought up in conversation many people will tune you out almost automatically. I found this true recently on a book tour. I was in Chicago and I called a bookstore to inquire as to whether or not my latest book, *Sex Begins in the Kitchen*, was in. A woman clerk answered the phone and I asked, "Do you have *Sex Begins in the Kitchen?*" After a short pause this woman literally screamed into the phone, "Where I have sex is none of your business." She hung up on me. I must admit I didn't even have the courage to call her back. All she heard was the word *sex* and she drew an instant inference and tuned me out.

There are many reasons why we have tuned out the word *masturbation*. One reason is that the term itself comes from two latin words that mean "to pollute with hand." It doesn't even sound like a nice thing to do, does it? But one thing you can pretty much count on is the fact that your adolescent will indeed masturbate. When I was young we used to say that 90 percent of the guys masturbated and the other 10 percent were liars.

Masturbation, of course, is self-stimulation, "playing with yourself" as the kids would say. I think another negative association with masturbation comes from the fact that many moms extinguish the natural tendency for a youngster to touch their genitalia with their hands. Many an adult can remember their mom or dad shouting, "Get your hands off your thing!" Of course there are many myths that have always accompanied the subject of masturbation. Myths like, "Your penis will fall off," or, "You'll go blind by Tuesday"; "Your head will be covered with zits within 24 hours"; "Your supply of semen will run out"; "You'll get a bad case of dementia praecox"; "You won't be able to have a baby," are just a few that have been with us for some time.

Can you imagine what the child thinks when, through personal curiosity and experimentation in adolescence, he or she learns that gently touching and caressing the genitalia is especially fulfilling? I can almost hear that young adolescent saying, "Hey, this isn't so bad after all."

Masturbation is one way adolescents can safely and, without harm to anyone, relieve their sexual pressures. Now remember that God created us in such a way that we have the capacity for those special feelings. Most adolescents report that their parents did not prepare them for the eventuality of a nocturnal emission—or a wet dream. A young male will have wet dreams in the absence of masturbation during the adolescent years. It's a very natural way for the body to rid itself of the extra semen that accumulates in the young male. Can you imagine the guilties a young male might get if his first nocturnal emission comes and he has not been prepared for its eventuality by either parent? It's important for us to realize that kids are going to have sexual thoughts during adolescence. They might be doing some fantasizing and masturbating; that is all part of growing up.

Although parents in many circles, particularly Christian circles, have made masturbation a controversy, I personally don't feel that it's one of the biggies in God's eyes. Jesus never did mention masturbation in the Bible. It is a normal part of every person's development. I don't see that masturbation causes any harm unless a person becomes overly preoccupied with it. Then it can contribute to an unhealthy thought life and feelings of guilt or lust. To help keep masturbation under control, kids need to avoid sexually stimulating movies, television programs, books, magazines, music, etc. as much as possible. They should also find other outlets—athletic activities, strenuous work, hobbies, etc.—for releasing the emotional tension caused by their sexual drives. Masturbation is a personal matter between individuals and God, but it is something each family is going to have to talk about. Kids will have to made a determination concerning masturbation based on their own feelings and experiences and what they think is part of God's will in their own lives.

I believe we ought to be acutely aware of the probability that our children are going to masturbate during their adolescent years. Be particularly sensitive to your children's privacy. If the door to the bathroom or bedroom is closed or locked, respect his time to himself without bugging him. Kids need time to themselves, just as their parents do.

Adolescents Long for Freedom

Someone asked me not too long ago, "How do you really know when your child begins adolescence?" Of course I think many people equate the beginning of adolescence with the beginning of the maturation process, that is, the time when our children begin to develop into young men and women. I responded that perhaps even a better way to tell whether or not your child is entering adolescence is to be very sensitive to the first time your 11- or 12-year-old sinks into the car seat as you drive past some kids on the corner. Many parents can recall when they began to give their parents vibes that they wished Mom or Dad wasn't around. This is the beginning of the desire to be free from parental restraint.

Ask a child sometime, "What age would you be if you could be any age at all?" What do you suppose most kids respond with? The most typical age children want to be is 16. Why 16? What's so special about 16? Well, for one thing they can drive. That's a biggy. Driving represents independence. In the teenager's life today the car is certainly close to being number one. That's one reason why I suggest that, when disciplining teenagers, parents zero in on three things: the car, money and privileges. Those are three things that the American teenager relates to almost without exception.

Adolescence is a time for that longing to be free. It's that very uncomfortable, uncertain time in a person's life when he is neither fish or fowl; in between the innocence of childhood and the awesome responsibility of facing the reality of adult life.

Arthur Fonzerelli, better known as the "Fonz," portrayed by Henry Winkler on "Happy Days," is a particularly popular person with the peer group. Why? The Fonz is cool. And more importantly, the Fonz doesn't have any parents. You never see Mr. and Mrs. Fonzerelli on a program. The Fonz doesn't report to anybody. He's free. The free spirit Fonz represents on "Happy Days" is what many teenagers long for. But they aren't free. They have moms and dads who tell them what to do and what not to do; they have younger brothers and sisters who drive them up the wall; teachers who just don't understand and are boring and give terrible assignments; girlfriends and boyfriends who, from one day to another, can't make up their minds whether they like them or not. So although the longing to be free is great with teenagers, they aren't very free. They are restricted. This lack of freedom is one reason why some teenagers rebel.

Kelly, age 15, is such a case. She came to me at the suggestion of her parents who were concerned about the changes they were seeing in Kelly's life. Kelly's mom was a home-ec teacher, a perfectionistic, a rather high-strung woman, and very overprotective of Kelly. As president of the PTA she had very definite ideas about child rearing, and very definite ideas about Kelly, the youngest of her three children.

Kelly's dad was an easygoing, laid-back professional person. A dentist, he found himself with a very heavy work load. He was very good at keeping his emotions to himself. Kelly's dad had enjoyed the serenity of their home with the two older sons, now 22 and 18. The older brother was in law school and the other was a freshman in the university.

Kelly was very perceptive and sensitive as to how she should act to please her mother. In fact, Kelly told me she thought her whole life was mapped out for her by her mother, that her mom knew exactly what she should be when she got older, what to study, who to date, as well as what dress looked best on her.

Kelly's parents' concern for her was justified—they only wished they had come for family counseling two years earlier when Kelly had started to ditch classes. Kelly was described by her mom and dad as a manipulator, outgoing, an excellent student who was cute, self-centered and lazy.

At age 14 Kelly showed an inordinate desire to be with young men. She started dating older guys. This of course met with much resistance from Mom and Dad.

But, like many parents faced with a kid's constant pleas, they finally gave in. Kelly began a downward slide very quickly as her fifteenth birthday approached. She became rebellious to the point of being openly defiant to her parents. Out of the blue she displayed a smart mouth as well as language that wasn't fit for the saltiest of sailors. Mom (remember she's the PTA president) started to get a series of calls from school. Not only was Kelly's ditching increasing, but she would show up at school dead drunk, when she did come in, at her 8:30 morning class! Mom and Dad sought professional help for Kelly when school officials caught her in the back seat of a car making out with a 19-year-old student.

As I met with Kelly in therapy, it became very clear that there was no way Mom was going to control her life. Kelly was going to show her folks that she was no longer the little girl they wanted her to be. She described her parents as terribly overprotective, archaic, old-fashioned, unrealistic and boring. She said she was the only one of her friends who had a curfew of 12:00 on weekends. Kelly's whole life-style seemed to say that she counted in life only when she controlled, when she won and when she bossed her parents around.

I must confess there were times when I felt helpless due to Kelly's great desire to be the opposite of what her mom wanted her to be. Her mom was not very good at following my advice to back off and give Kelly some room, so Kelly was going to show her. And show her she did! But at what expense! Kelly began a pattern of staying out past her curfew. The more she rebelled the more Mom and Dad tried to clamp down. Finally, one night she just didn't come home at all. At age 15 she left home for a period of some 13 months. Of course she was forced to quit school. During this period of time she lost almost all contact with her school friends and found a new group to associate with, some crusty-looking fellows who didn't work regularly and rode motorcycles for enjoyment.

During these 13 months away Kelly was transformed from a relatively naive and sweet young lady into a hard and abused young lady. She went, in short order, from drinking a few beers a day to smoking so much pot that—in her own words—she was so wasted she could hardly see straight.

She finally moved in with three young men, ages 19-22; shared a one-bedroom apartment with them. During this period of time she had many sexual experiences not only with the three men she lived with, but with several others as well. She was used in the truest sense of the word. In the 13-month period she got pregnant on two occasions, had two abortions, and the last guy she "went with" left town as soon as he heard he was going to be a father. He was a coke-head and had already fathered two children by age 21.

After 13 months of freedom, Kelly began to make some overtures about coming home. She called me at my office one day and caught me by surprise. I was with a client but took the time to speak with her when I learned it was Kelly on the phone. She asked, "Can I see you?" I said, "Of course you can." And we set up an appointment for that afternoon.

When Kelly walked into the office, I couldn't quite believe my eyes. Where had the blonde-haired, blue-eyed, pretty little 15-year-old gone to? What I saw before me was frightening. She looked rough, beaten-down, and her language was atrocious. She obviously had very little self-respect at that point in her life. I asked her quite directly if she had had it with her new freedom, wasn't it really time to go home. As she sobbed in my office she nodded her head; she thought it was time to go home.

I called Kelly's parents and they came to the office

and the four of us spent the afternoon talking about many of the same issues we had talked about a year earlier: responsibilities, curfews, language, smoking, drinking, pot-smoking, and her general demeanor. We began to make an agreement that both parties could live by.

It was a great personal joy for me to see Kelly want to go home and live with her mom and dad. After all, they were the two people who loved her most in all this world. As I saw them leave the office that afternoon, arm-in-arm, I knew it wasn't going to be easy. It was going to be very difficult to put things together and to heal a relationship that had been so broken. Since then I have spent several hours with Kelly, talking about how special she is and about her need to treat herself as special if she was ever going to be in a position to attract people who are good for her, people who have good self-concepts, who would be less likely to create situations where Kelly would continually be used and abused.

Since that time Kelly is living a fairly normal life as a teenager. She's back in school and is essentially allowing her parents to parent her. She doesn't always like it. There're still some hassles to be solved. But basically the relationship is healing.

I asked Kelly, if she could tell teenagers one thing, what would it be? What would be her personal advice to others her own age and in the same situation of rebellion. She offered two things: first, try to realize even though your parents seem out of it they really do love you and care about what happens to you; second, stick it out at home no matter how bad it is. Living out there in the world by yourself is the pits.

Perhaps you're thinking that Kelly is an extreme case; let me assure you she isn't. I have case histories, many of which are very similar to Kelly's, with many of the same hurts, trials, tribulations and with basically the same results. Given time, teenagers learn that there isn't a better place on earth than home.

I wish I had a nickel for every time someone has commented to me something along the line of, "Why do you continually bring up God in your book?" In fact, I've been told by many people that they would have *really* enjoyed my book if I had just left God out of it completely. I usually comment that "I feel I ought to talk about God since I really am using His book as the prime resource for my writings." I'm always amazed at how startled people seem at that response. But God does give us direction for a hurting world, doesn't He? In Kelly's case, for example, there're some beautiful Scriptures that could have prevented the many hurts in Kelly's life if she and her mom and dad had really followed God's directions.

Listen to what the psalmist says about God's laws: "God's laws are perfect. They protect us, make us wise, and give us joy and light. God's laws are pure, eternal, just. They are more desirable than gold. They are sweeter than honey dripping from a honeycomb. For they warn us away from harm and give success to those who obey them" (Ps. 19:7-11).

Paul, in his letter to the Ephesians, said, "Children, obey your parents; this is the right thing to do because God has placed them in authority over you. Honor your father and mother. This is the first of God's Ten Commandments that ends with a promise. And this is the promise: that if you honor your father and mother, yours will be a long life, full of blessing" (6:1-3).

Without a doubt, if Kelly had honored her father and mother she wouldn't have gotten into the terrible mess she got herself into. But the Scripture continues with some good advice for parents. "And now a word to you parents. Don't keep on scolding and nagging your children, making them angry and resentful. Rather, bring them up with the loving discipline the Lord himself approves, with suggestions and godly advice" (v. 4). The part of that verse that really jumps out of the page to me is the part about "don't scold and nag your children, making them angry and resentful."

Kelly was one angry and resentful young lady who wanted her freedom from a mom who had to make all her decisions for her.

Chapter 2

Everybody's Doing It, Doing It, Doing It!

To what extent will young people go to be accepted by the group?

I believe that one of the most frightening things for parents is the realization of what awesome power the peer group has over our own children. Think about it. Here you've put everything you could into rearing this kid the way you think he ought to be reared. You thought you provided him with adequate models; you've tried to communicate, talk with him, care for him the best you could. But even the best parent, doing the best possible job, has a hard time thwarting the effects and sheer power of the peer group.

God's Word tells us, "Don't copy the behavior and customs of this world" (Rom. 12:2). Now there's an easy assignment, right? Adolescents try desperately to show their peers that they do copy, that they do accept the mores and the standards of the masses. In fact, recently I worked with a young man who had done a 180-degree turnaround in school—he'd gone from an A student to a failing student. When we got down to where the rubber meets the road we found out that this abrupt change in behavior occurred because of the tremendous amount of pressure he felt to get poor grades in school. He was an outcast because he had chosen to do well in school and gain good grades.

Dr. James Dobson, in his book *Preparing for Adolescence*, talks about a very famous experiment in social psychology. Psychologists wanted to study the effect of peer pressure on teenage subjects.

In the well-conceived and well-designed study, 10 teenagers were told that they were going to view cards with straight lines on them. They were going to vote by way of raised hands for the longest line. However, nine of the teenagers were told to vote for the second longest line, not the longest line, contrary to the instructions given. The tenth teenager was not let in on these instructions, so there was really only one guinea pig—the one who wasn't told to vote for the second longest line.

Can you imagine the look on the guinea pig's face when nine hands went up in the air, voting for the second longest line? Even though it was obvious that the line was not the longest, out of fear that he'd be different, the guinea pig slowly, hesitantly raised his hand, but he did raise his hand and agree with the group. He didn't have the power of his convictions, even though he knew he was right, to say that the group was wrong.[5]

Now you might be thinking, "Yes, but that's an isolated case. Most people wouldn't do that." Not according to this study. More than 75 percent of the guinea pigs responded in the very same way. This classical social study gives us parents insight into the profound effect group pressure has upon our adolescents.

Do you remember the time in elementary school when you knew the right answer to a question the teacher asked but didn't put your hand up? Why? Out of fear that maybe there was a chance in a million that you might be wrong and you'd look ridiculous to your peers. The fear of rejection is so great in some of us that we won't even try, even when we know the right answer.

Okay. So what does this say to us as parents? What can we do to help encourage our children to take a stand on whatever their beliefs are?

Encourage Nurturing a Best Friend

I believe that one of the things we as parents can do is to really reinforce and encourage that one special friendship our son or daughter might have. An adolescent's best friends are probably going to be of the same sex. And with a little help from you in nurturing that relationship, your teenager will discover a special bond between himself and a friend, someone who will support him when he is faced with a decision that might go against the peer group standards.

If you have elementary school age children at home and they go to a public school, it might be a good idea to give them the opportunity to invite some of their other friends from their church to spend the night with them, to spend the weekend with your family, perhaps to go on a family outing with you. It is important for children to realize at an early age that their church friends do not have to be once- or twice-a-week friends, that they can develop a close and intimate relationship even though they live several miles from one another. But, without our support and encouragement, the likelihood of this relationship growing is slight.

With the hectic pace of today's activities, it is easy for couples to suddenly discover that they have been parents for 15 years and literally haven't done a great deal with their children. Once the parents get their careers developed to a point where they can spend some time with their adolescents, the adolescents are beginning to be at a point where they no longer enjoy doing things with just Mommy and Daddy and at this point, the peer group has taken over.

It may not be too late. Encourage your son or daughter to take a friend along on a family weekend. This will go a long way in strengthening the relationship between the adolescent and their friends. At the same time it will give the family the experience of doing some things together.

Be More Obvious in Your Influence

How many hours a day do you spend with your children? Two? One? Sometimes only a few minutes a day? In this hectic world it's easy for parents and kids to be isolated from one another. And when we might have time on weekends to spend with our kids our activity-conscious society fills our schedules to such an extent that no time is provided for the family. We talk a great deal about the "quality" time we give our kids as opposed to quantity time; but, really, all your kids understand is "time." They just need to be with you, to observe your life day in and day out. Of course this puts a great burden on parents to monitor their own lives.

I believe it's a wise parent who tells his kids what he believes and why he believes it. But, above all, it's wiser to *show* what he believes by his life. It does no good—or very little good—for a parent to lecture on the evils of smoking or drinking while he himself freely indulges in those things.

When I think of the influence we have on our kids' lives I think of a woman I'll call Sally. Sally had a 17-year-old named Sarah. Sarah was a very popular girl in her school. She was a pom-pom girl and an attendant in the queen's court at her school's homecoming celebration.

Due to her God-given beauty, inside as well as outside, Sarah never lacked for dates. And to top that off she was a fine student.

One day Sally, Sarah's mother, answered the door. Sarah's 17-year-old boyfriend was standing there. He asked if he could come in. Of course Sarah's mom said, "Sure, come on in and have a seat."

Well, Bob, Sarah's boyfriend, started off the conversation by saying, "Mrs. J., what is it with Sarah? How come I'm not getting any?"

Now I'm telling you, if any guy ever comes to my house and knocks on my front door and asks me, regarding my daughter, "How come I'm not getting any?" may the good Lord have mercy on his soul as I consider stringing him up on my front porch and plucking his eyes from his head one at a time!

Sally was, of course, taken aback and shocked by what she just heard and couldn't quite believe it. But she looked at Bob and said, "You and I have to talk." (As hard as this might seem to believe, this conversation actually took place.) Sarah's mom went right after Bob. She started out, "When I was 17 I hated sauerkraut, despised it. I couldn't stand the smell of it. It made me want to vomit just to think about it. Today I'm 41 years old and I love sauerkraut. There's not a thing I love more in the world than sauerkraut.

"Now as you know, my daughter and I have a good relationship. We talk about a lot of things. In fact, I know that my daughter is planning on breaking up with you tonight. The reason is that she is sick and tired of your constant harassing her for sex. I think, Bob, that what my daughter's trying to tell you is that she's not ready for sex. And we hope that when the day comes when she is ready, that she will be married. I know that's how she feels right now. She's telling you plainly and clearly that she doesn't like sauerkraut and she wants no part of sauerkraut in her life now. And because of your imma-ture attitude toward her feelings she's ready to kiss you off."

Now if you don't think those words took Bob back a few paces, you're wrong.

Sarah didn't "kiss him off" and on another occasion, as conversation developed along the same topic, Bob shared with Sarah's mom that he felt all kinds of pressure from the other guys in his peer group. Every time, after a date with Sarah, when he saw the group the following morning at school, they asked 20 questions as to how far he got. "Did you get to first base? Second base? Third base? Hit a home run?" The interesting thing is that with the insight given by this wise mom, Bob was able to back off, in spite of peer pressure. When Bob got it straight in his head that Sarah didn't want any part of premarital sex, their relationship turned around 180 degrees. Bob was able to resist the pressure from his peer group; he took the pressure off Sarah and the two became *more intimate,* if you will, in the truest sense of the word. They could enjoy each other's company and have fun together. They truly liked each other, especially when the hassles and strains were removed from their relationship.

Think how good the relationship had to be between mother and daughter. If I had the authority or the oppor-tunity to give a mother-of-the-year award, it would go to this mom, this mom who resisted the temptation to tear out that young man's spleen and, instead sat down to give him some good, wise counsel when he really needed it. How great it would be if every parent could really talk about everything with his or her adolescent. We as par-ents get very few shots at them as they are growing up. They seem to grow too quickly. We don't seem to have enough time along the way to share with them what's really important in our lives. But when we dig down deep and share out of our own personal lives with our children, that's when we really give carte blanche for them to discuss with us anything they want to. Such a relationship doesn't come naturally. It takes work, hard work, a lot of listening, and a great deal of understanding and a lot of mutual respect and love between parent and child to get to that point.

Your teenager needs your positive influence in his life.

Select His Environment

How much time do your children spend in school? A good guess might be between six and seven hours each day. Here's an area where parents really need to put some thought: Where do you want your children to go to school?

It's no secret that private, parochial and Christian school enrollments are surging. Why? Well, there're obviously many reasons, but one answer for sure is that many parents believe the public school system does a beautiful job of teaching irresponsibility; that there is little discipline, closeness or warmth between teacher and child; and too many things are going on in the public schools that are negative influences on our kids. However, if you decide to send your child to a Christian school you had better make the decision in his first grade.

If you start talking about sending your child to a Christian school as late as fourth grade, he's going to say, "No, I don't want to go. I don't want to leave my friends." Even by the fourth grade friendships are already established and the peer group is in full swing. I believe that if you want your child to have a private school education you have to make that decision as early in the child's education as possible to maximize the influence of the school's environment.

It sounds easy at this point, doesn't it? All you have to do is pick the closest Christian school for your children, or go the public school route. Well, it's not that easy. Suppose you choose to send your child to a Christian school. You better take a long, hard look at the great variety of Christian and private schools available in your community. If your community is like most (larger communities), there are great differences in Christian schools.

Too many Christian schools teach a negative Christianity, one that's filled with "thou shalt nots," with little emphasis on the "thou shalts." As a result too many young people come out of Christian schools with a very poor image of God the Father. Too many of them don't see God as the loving Father; rather, He's the guy in the sky with the biggest Whammo slingshot ever. So, parents, if you are interested enough to consider a Christian education for your children, I hope that you are interested enough to get yourself down to the school, while school is in session, with your son or daughter in tow, to observe and get a feel for how things are going to be at the particular school you are considering.

A school should not only provide adequate education and meaningful worship time together, but it should also give ample opportunity for social interaction among students. But some of these Christian schools are like some of our churches. I think of a Saturday evening when we invited the young people from our own church to our home. We had expressly invited them to our home with the sponsors because we had, among other things, two jukeboxes in our home. We thought the kids would really enjoy a "fifties party." So the kids came dressed in fifties style and they were about to begin dancing with one another. Suddenly one of the sponsors, a young seminary student, issued an edict that there would be no dancing. He had his personal convictions but I felt he was wrong. If the church doesn't provide opportunity for kids to fellowship with one another socially within the office of the church, there're certainly all kinds of opportunities outside the church. I know, as a parent with two daughters and a son, I'd certainly much rather have my kids in a church member's home, dancing to fifties and sixties rock-'n'-roll records than have them out on the town doing what I know teenagers do with frequency.

One study of youth groups in both Protestant and Catholic churches revealed that only about six percent of those in church youth groups stayed in the church as adults.[6] That's a sad commentary on the church's effectiveness at meeting the needs of hurting Christians. So if we're not reaching teenagers, perhaps the church can be held directly responsible, in part, for not providing avenues for young people to socialize and fellowship with other young people.

In my seminars throughout the country I get to meet many pastors, and get at least a glimpse into their church ministries. My observation is this: the churches that are growing by leaps and bounds are churches that have (1) a women's ministry—particularly a women's Bible study, (2) a singles' ministry, and (3) a very active young people's group which usually has music as a very integral part of their ministry. These churches also have (4) a discipleship program. All of these "programs" in the church are really designed, I think, to deal with the realities of living in a world such as ours.

People need to be fed. Young people need to be fed, and not only by God's Word, but also through frequent contact with others in similar situations who are also working at maturing. The Pharisees are still with us. They are those who feel that young people shouldn't be happy, that they shouldn't be able to enjoy social functions together. Too many of us focus on the laws, the rules, and the regulations rather than on the fact of God's love for each of us and His plan for our lives.

If our adolescents are going to deal with a world that says, "Conform, be like everybody else," then our teenagers must see positive relationships in their family, in their church life, and in their school life; relationships that seem to say that Almighty God really does care about us and that living Christian lives is exciting and not all dull. A Christian life is not just a Wednesday evening, Sunday morning life. It's a 24-hour-a-day life. A life that's filled with goodness, peace, love and enjoyment of one another.

Investigate the school you are considering sending your child to. Make sure, if it's a Christian school, that it really provides everything your child needs. Because he's going to spend more of his waking hours in schools, being influenced by his teachers and his peers, than he is going to spend around you. If you choose not to send him to a Christian school, for whatever reason, then make sure his non-school hours are spent in the presence of those people and influences you want to affect his life; if you don't make your influence obvious and early, someone else will.

Help Him Adjust to Change

Change affects everyone, but change seems to be particularly stressful to adolescents. Parents have to help their teenagers cope with change; yet, many times the parents are also trying to adjust to the same changes.

Richard came to me a few years ago because he was in great difficulty—he was in trouble with the law. He had just partaken in an armed robbery and admitted to recently participating in 16 home burglaries.

Richard was 17 and the oldest child in his family. His mom, at the time Richard came for therapy, was seeking dissolution of her marriage of 22 years. Now I'm not about to say that if Richard's parents weren't going through a divorce, but had a good, sound marriage, that Richard wouldn't have gotten into trouble. I'm not *going* to say it, but I'm tempted to; tempted because it came out in therapy with Richard. The most powerful feelings he had inside of him were the feelings concerning his mom and dad's impending divorce.

I really believe Richard felt that life was being unfair to him, that basically life had kicked him square in the teeth. Therefore, in a democratic society, if life had the right to kick him in the teeth, then he was going to strike out.

Not only was Richard going through a change because of his parents' divorce, but the family had just moved from the Boston area to the Southwest. Of course, breaking into a new peer group is a very difficult assignment for some kids, and it was with Richard. He had to become acquainted with what his peers in this new setting expected of him. He had to reestablish himself in a whole new environment. Although he was an athlete, his sport wasn't played until spring, so he couldn't use baseball as a way of initiating friendships. So Richard felt very isolated and lonely. These two changes in his life really laid the foundation for peer pressure. The need to conform made Richard, who was a pretty good kid, become involved in some things that were very uncharacteristic of his prior life.

One of the other guys who was involved in the armed robbery had, by chance, been sitting next to Richard in a class and had introduced himself—there was a friend. It may not have been the friend Richard would have picked if he had been able to sit back and pick his friends, but it was somebody, somebody to be close to. So here's this kid, a pretty good kid who had never been in any difficulty in his life, being pressured into driving the getaway car for an armed robbery, as well as being party to 16 home burglaries.

Adolescents need help in coping with change.

Self-Esteem—Second Verse, Same as the First

You know, it's hard to say no. It takes a lot of character and a lot of self-esteem to do what we know we should.

When I was a little kid, my friend Moonhead and I would walk along the village roads in the summertime, anxiously watching for a driver to flip a cigarette butt out of a window of a passing car. We'd run to get the cigarette butt that we didn't even need matches for. I'm sure we smoked for lots of reasons—to seem like big boys, to impress our peers, to feel more grown up, older than we were. The first time I ever smoked a cigarette I was seven years old, and I continued smoking until I got smart and quit at approximately 22. (It was also about the same time I met my wife—in the men's room of a local hospital. But that's a long story we don't have time to get into yet.)

As a teenager I really didn't know how harmful cigarettes are to us. There was some talk about how destructive smoking was; today it's even spelled out on the package: "Warning: The Surgeon General has determined that cigarette smoking is harmful to your health." Yet even though it's right on the carton people still smoke by the millions. So although we know things aren't good for us we continue to do some of those things. It's hard to say no.

Even when we become adults it's hard to do what we should. For example, which day of the week do you suppose is the most popular to start a diet on? Mondays, right? Why Mondays? Because Monday, being the first day of the working week, makes it easy on Saturday night to lie to ourselves as we reach for that second piece of pie and say, "Monday I'm going on a diet." Even though we know that all that sugar isn't good for us, even though we know we shouldn't smoke cigarettes, we as adults have a terrible time saying no. Imagine, then, the difficulty adolescents have, with peer pressure as strong as it is, saying no to one hit on a marijuana cigarette. It's extremely difficult. My experience with teenagers is that they consciously know that many of the things they do are really not good for them, but they don't have the self-esteem to reject them.

Parents must help their children build a good self-esteem. When we feel good about ourselves, when we can accept the real us, just as we are, then growing up becomes much easier. If we can't have a good self-image then we are headed for a great deal of trouble. We will never really feel that we are worthwhile, that we belong.

There are some grim statistics that highlight the over-powering need for adolescents to belong. If an adolescent doesn't feel that he belongs and has his place, or if he feels rejected by society, that adolescent might end up a tragic statistic. Today, in our country, 13 teenagers will kill themselves. The suicide rate among 15- 24-year-olds has risen by almost 300 percent in the last 20 years.[7]

There are those who think that as many as 500,000 teenagers attempt suicide in a given year. I believe that many of the teenagers who kill themselves do so because they feel that they really can't measure up in this world. The sad thing is, by my observation, many teenagers who have taken their lives were actually extremely good students in school and were very highly thought of by others. However, the important thing, remember, is how they saw themselves. Maybe they felt that they were unworthy or nothing. They may have grown up in an environment where Dad pushed the level of expectation so high that the teenager was defeated by the overly-high demands placed upon him. Or, to get Mom and Dad off the hook, perhaps the child placed these high expectations on himself. I haven't seen any suicide statistics among firstborn children or only children, but I wouldn't be surprised to find that there was an extremely high incidence of suicide among firstborn children because of their perfectionistic nature.

In an article on adolescent suicide, McHenry, Tishler and Christman studied the behavior of adolescents who attempted suicide. The majority of these evidenced the following changes: (1) drastic changes in personal appearance from good to bad; (2) somatic complaints (stomachache, backache, headache, diarrhea, etc.); (3) inability to concentrate; (4) dramatic shifts in the quality of their school work; (5) changes in daily behavioral patterns which could manifest themselves in extreme fatigue, excessive sleeping, withdrawal, decreased appetite, emotional outbursts, use of alcohol and drugs, loss of friends, and an overwhelming sense of guilt and shame.

The investigators also cited crises which are accompanied by the aforementioned behavioral changes: the death of a family member, relative or close friend; separation of parents, siblings or relatives; personal problems with the law or someone close having problems with the law; plus others.

The writers suggest that discussing suicide will not make the depressed adolescent more inclined to do so; rather, he is emotionally relieved by the opportunity to discuss his feelings.[8]

I know it is downright scary even to think about teenage suicide. I really believe we could prevent such tragedies in our teens' lives if we would dedicate ourselves to honest communication with them. That is, when we get brave enough to share some of *our* thoughts and feelings with our children, it gives *them* permission to discuss their feelings and attitudes. Remember, prior to the teen years, plant the seed in your adolescent's mind that the coming years may be stormy ones. There might be a time when your teenager is tempted to withdraw and keep to himself and experience some weird and crazy and upsetting feelings. With the planting of that seed, the teenager might be able to ward off some feelings of desolation and loneliness and be able to follow through on the pact that parent and teenager have made—that is that we'll always be able to discuss problems and feelings.

Chapter 3

Dating, Mating and Waiting

Many times I've been asked at my seminars throughout the country, "Okay, Leman, when are you going to let *your* daughters date?"

I reply, very matter-of-factly, "When they're 31. And of course on a double date with their mother in the back seat."

Since time began, girls and boys have always been drawn together like moths to a flame. However, in many traditional cultures dating was never an option because the parents of the children chose their future mates. But in our society dating is a very appropriate way to get to know which qualities you are looking for in a lifetime mate.

Now I believe that teenagers should be intimate in their dating—but not physically intimate. As a young man begins to date one young lady more than any others his goal should be to discover as many things about her, and she about him, as they each can. How does she think about certain things? Can he share some of his own burdens and hurts with her? Can he take off his mask and let her see the real him without getting that feeling of rejection?

Why should kids date, anyway? Is it really important? I think it's important. But there are several factors that have to be considered.

Dating

From what I have discovered in working with families, many kids start dating because their parents push them into it, sometimes at a very early age.

Have you ever heard an adult say to a seven-year-old child—maybe even to your child—"Do you have a girlfriend (boyfriend) yet?" Now what does this convey to the youngster? "Gee, it sounds like I'm supposed to get a girlfriend already."

From my observation, children in some circles are being forced to grow up too early. Too much too quickly seems to be in vogue in modern-day America. Parents and peers literally force the young boy or girl to concentrate on "boyfriend" or "girlfriend" rather than just "friends." Kids need to spend several years developing friends of both sexes.

Teens or even preteens often begin dating because of peer pressure. What kids their own age feel and think during the turbulent years of adolescence usually outweighs what Mom and Dad think. So even if you never encouraged dating as your kids were growing up, by the time they are in junior high school dating is becoming very critical to them because of peer pressure. This age has a need for status, to be seen with the right person. There is very little emotional feeling for the date, just a desire to be seen with someone. This is very closely linked to the teenager's self-esteem. The someone he dates—or would like to—has to look "good"—a neat hairstyle, good physical appearance, and "cool." But, unless he meets those standards himself, he won't find anyone to date him. And this is where many young people meet head-on with an identity crisis. They really want someone to notice them.

Everybody, at any age, wants to be noticed. Nobody wants to be neutral, invisible, a non-person. But this desire to want people to notice us is particularly strong during the adolescent years.

When I was a college sophomore I got myself in hot water with school officials. One evening the ice cream machine in the dorm where I lived went on the blink and began to give away freebees. All us good Christian students went down and proceeded to rip off the machine. Of course the dorm lost a lot of money in the course of the evening. The head resident, who was an ordained pastor, put up a sign near the switchboard to the effect that "All of you who participated in the unauthorized ice cream social the other evening, please put your money in this box because the dorm lost x amount of dollars."

My roommate and I came in, saw the sign and the money, and also saw the old gentleman who sat at the switchboard, sound asleep. We looked at each other with the same thought, *Wouldn't it be funny if we ripped off the conscience fund?* Well, we ripped it off alright, and like most 19-year-old kids who do something to be noticed, we had to tell the whole world. So we told the whole world by throwing a party for the guys in our wing. It didn't take very long for the word to get down to the head resident and on to the dean of students that Leman and his roommate were responsible for ripping off the conscience fund.

Teenagers have a need to be noticed. They will go to great lengths to be noticed by the peer group, especially the opposite sex. They reason, "How will I get dates if nobody sees me?"

I was curious about the dating habits of college students. So while I was at the University of Arizona campus I did a survey to determine just how many students dated at least once a week in the dorm system. I discovered that a surprisingly low 15 percent of the college students dated on a regular basis. One might think that on a college campus of 35,000 students there would be all kinds of opportunities to date. Although they daily walk by literally thousands of members of the opposite sex, they have very little opportunity to really be noticed or get to meet someone.

Now I personally think that by the time an adolescent reaches college age he should really be dating. So I encouraged the students I worked with to meet people. I'll never forget one experience I had. Four young coeds, who had heard me speak at freshman orientation, took me up on my invitation to come visit me in my office if I could be of service to them. They were all a little apprehensive because they didn't know what to expect. But one young woman who seemed to be the spokesperson for the group popped off about not being able to meet any men on our campus. Well, I explained to them that there was a big difference between high school and college and now they would have to take things into their own hands and sort of create the kind of environment that would attract the type of boys they were looking for.

I asked them if they would be willing to do something a little crazy. They looked at each other inquisitively and gave a halfhearted shrug of their shoulders, which I took to mean that they were willing. I suggested that they take a popcorn popper to one of our largest men's residence halls, go into the lobby, sit down and begin popping corn.

You can imagine their feelings, thoughts and expressions as they walked into Santa Cruz Hall on the University of Arizona campus, complete with popcorn popper, oil, butter, popcorn, some bowls and a sheet to spread out on the floor. They told me they kept looking at each other as if to say, "I can't believe we're actually doing this. I feel so stupid." But they spread out the sheet, plugged in the popcorn popper and began to pop corn. As the popcorn aroma worked itself up the stairwell of the men's residence hall, about 40 guys, like bears awaking from a long winter's nap, lumbered toward the lobby area. Forty to four. Those aren't bad odds for anybody.

As it turned out the girls had a great time. And, boy, did they meet guys! Some of the guys thought it was a pretty good idea too because, as the evening wore on, four of them stayed around and paired up with these four young coeds and they ended up going out for pizza after the popcorn bash. The following evening these four guys retaliated with a popcorn party in the girls' dorm. So when dating begins to get critical you sometimes have to take matters into your own hands and create situations where you meet others. But be sure the situation is going to draw the kind of guys or girls you want to meet. You've heard about the singles who go to the singles bars to meet Mr. or Miss Right only to find out after they've met someone that that's all they want to do, hang around bars.

I can think of one young lady I recently worked with who tried to get men to notice her by hitchhiking. She got three men to notice her real well. They picked her up, took her off in the desert, beat her, robbed her of her money, forced her to perform several sex acts with them and then dumped her in the desert naked.

Teenagers want to be noticed. They want to think that they are special, above the norm. Yet by their very nature they see themselves as very awkward, gawky, uncoordinated and klutzy. Actually there is nothing wrong about being "ordinary." I think of the fact that God always uses ordinary people. In fact, the disciples were ordinary—a tax collector who was really the scum of the earth in his day, some smelly fishermen, and such. Sounds like a top-shelf group, doesn't it? Although many teenagers see themselves as awkward, unappreciated and lowly, Almighty God sees each of them as very special and has some great plans in store for all of us. If we will let Him, God will reveal Himself and His plans to each of us—whether we are "ordinary" people or very special in the eyes of the world.

I thought the movie *Oh God* was an excellent one. I found myself laughing and crying all through it. Many parts left me a little cold, others really took me soaring. One spot in particular I'd like to share with you. John Denver, an assistant manager of a grocery store, was approached by God, George Burns, to be his messenger to the world. In disbelief John Denver is wrestling with this very notion and he turns to God and asks, "But, God, why did you choose me? I don't even belong to a church." One of the classic lines of the movie was when God turned to John Denver and said, "Neither do I."

Each of us as Christians needs to be reminded that although we see ourselves as ordinary, God sees every one of us as special. He has a wonderful individual plan for every one of us. Parents should also see each of *their* children as very special, and treat them as special. They should spend time with them and show that they think their kids are special. It's in these early experiences that self-concept takes root.

It's important for a child to learn that he is good and capable and that Mom and Dad, brothers and sisters care for him. If we are able to create an environment within the home where a kid can grow and learn about himself and others without a constant fear of rejection or ridicule, then that growth can be positive.

So many times I see parents become tremendous flaw-pickers, pointing out all the shortcomings and faults of their teenagers. This kind of discouraging experience during those turbulent adolescent years can do nothing but drive the kid we love from our home and get him hooked into whatever's in vogue in the peer group. People often ask me, as I'm speaking across the country, why so many of my examples come from very young children. I do that because the training up of a child really occurs in the first seven years of his life. If we don't catch them then, chances are we never will. After all, teenagers can really do whatever they want to do in life. It's only out of respect and love that they allow us parents to parent them. The teenager who really wants to be rebellious and give his parents the hassle of their lifetime can certainly do so.

Now, let's get down to talking about dating regulations. What about dating? What's this whole area really all about? What is accomplished by dating? What are some of the guidelines for dating? When should a teenager begin to date?

Of course each individual kid is different, but I think 16 is a good age for a kid to begin dating one-on-one. I think in group dating situations kids can certainly be dating as early as 14 or 15, as long as they understand that dating is permissible at that early age only in group dating. There's a tremendous danger in letting teenagers begin dating too early. I had a 15-year-old girl tell me once that she was absolutely bored with dating. She started so young that she kept progressing further and further in order to keep the dating experience exciting. Now she was so sick of getting drunk, stoned, smashed and making out that she really had had it. She wanted time out from guys. She felt that she had been raked over the coals too many times during her first 15 years.

Dating, regardless of all the social problems of the peer group, should be a time of having fun, sharing time with somebody else and getting to know each other. But your teenager is going to need some help in setting guidelines. I believe the teenager in your home who is about to start dating should be encouraged to prepare his or her own guidelines for dating. Most kids basically know the problems that exist with dating, and most of them really do not want to get themselves in a situation they can't handle. So let them prepare a list of do's and don'ts. I think that's a far healthier way to start than for Mom and Dad to issue an edict on how things are going to be. One thing we know about young people is that if they have any input into rules and regulations there's a higher probability that they will adhere to those rules. Of course there will have to be some discussion between parents and kids concerning the list, and probably some give and take.

Too many young people try to make dating a purely sexual time together. They do this for many reasons, but the primary reason, I think, is again peer pressure. They are coerced into proving themselves. The sexual drive is there, but they must be taught that, like everything else in life, it should be put under control. The choice is rather clear: either we control our emotions or our emotions control us.

The tragedy of it all is that if young men really knew how young women felt about sex they'd be shocked. You see, the most special physical act according to women is not sex, but just to be physically held. Let's face it, there's going to be some kind of physical touching between a young guy and girl as they go through the dating process. They're going to be holding hands, kissing, touching in some way, shape or form. Many of them are going to be petting, and they're going to get into heavy petting and, as statistics tragically demonstrate to us, many of them will become involved in intercourse as well. But just as men don't understand women, and vice versa, so boys and girls don't understand each other's distinct needs and specialness either.

An article I read years ago really demonstrates for me the difference between young men and young women. The study was reported in *Psychology Today*. Researchers found, in a study of 432 young people, that teenage boys and girls looked at things quite differently from one another. Teenage girls who wore hip-hugging jeans and no bra tops thought they were just being stylish. But to the boys who looked at them their fashion suggested that the girls wanted to have sex.

Other conclusions of the study by four members of the Department of Psychology at UCLA found that both sexes agree that if a girl accepts a date with a guy who has a fast reputation, she should expect the boy to come on strong during their date. And interestingly enough, relative to my earlier comment about girls just liking to be physically held, they were more likely to agree with the statement, "Sometimes I wish girls could just be friends with boys without worrying about sexual relationships." Someone along the line really sold us a bill of goods about men and women being the same. Men and women will never be the same. We were created distinctly different by the Creator—which doesn't mean that we have less than equal social value. But the point is that men and women are different.

Dating for young Christian teenagers today is difficult, to say the least, in a world that really attacks the very center and sanctity of the special way in which we look at sex.

The dating experience can be a rocky one. There're

lots of hills and valleys. There're going to be many tears and heartaches, and ups and downs. But if teenagers are able to develop friendships with other kids who believe as they do, if they realize that they are special, and if they don't want to get themselves into situations where they're used or are using someone else, then I believe, with God's help and sheer determination on their part, teenagers can get through those tough times with minimal scrapes and scars.

As I told a couple of parents just a few months ago, our goal with teenagers is to be able to get them through the teenage years without them killing themselves or without someone else killing them. It's difficult to be different, especially when the whole peer group says everybody's got to be the same. But if your son or daughter really wants somebody special in life, if they really look forward to marriage as being something super special where two really do come together and become an entity within themselves, a loving relationship that is nurtured with mutual respect and love, then they're going to have to have the courage to be different, to speak their mind, to learn to say no and to be very selective about whom they date and with whom they associate.

Mating

We've already said a bit about premarital sex. There's a great deal of pressure on teenagers to engage in premarital sex. This comes not only from the peer group but from society in general. Kids are forced to grow up too soon, and to complicate matters, every place we look teenagers are being bombarded by the media with all different forms of sexuality. Advertisers have learned that, unfortunately, sex sells. But as a marriage and family counselor, I don't think we can say too much. In the first place, the Bible has a great deal to say about sex. However, let's forget, for a minute, the many scriptural admonitions against fornication and adultery and concentrate on the very prevalent health hazards posed by premarital sex.

I know you've probably heard a lot of statistics about the problems young people encounter because they engage in intercourse before they're married. But let me refresh your memory.

In this day, sexually active young people can get advice on birth control methods without ever letting their parents know about it. But as the experts tell us, many young people don't even use birth control when available. There are probably several reasons for this. The first reason is very difficult for adults to understand: many a young woman who feels alienated and unloved by the significant others in her life—her mom and dad and her family—might really want to get pregnant. The fantasy of having her own little baby sounds wonderfully attractive to a young teenager who feels that life has dealt her an unfair hand of one kind or another. Such teenage naiveté is only exceeded by her stupidity. It's only after that young adolescent has given birth to a child that she begins to realize the awesome responsibilities she has incurred by choosing to get pregnant. So even though it's a common assumption about how young men are always looking for young women to score on, let it be known that there are many young women who are looking for just the right young man to father their first child.

Another reason why many girls do not use birth control methods is that they were brought up with traditional Judeo-Christian values. It might be a very guilt-producing experience for them to practice birth control because it's as if they are planning to sin or to go against God's laws. I recall one young woman of 16 years of age who was very sexually active with her boyfriend of 18.

Although the young man always wanted to practice contraception by use of a condom, she wouldn't let him, for it would violate her religious practices.

I suppose the most obvious reason teenagers don't practice birth control is that many of them simply don't live a very structured or planned life. In the process of not taking the time to think about what their physical and sexual limits are in the dating relationship, many teenagers find themselves in situations where one thing just leads to another. In the height of romantic love it's very difficult and cumbersome to take time out to use contraceptives of any kind. There is a tendency in some teenagers to be so caught up in the fantasy of lovemaking that they don't want any interruptions, even that of protecting themselves from pregnancy. Did you ever see a movie where, during one of those titillating love scenes, the young lover stopped to use a contraceptive? It just doesn't seem like the romantic thing to do.

We need to reinforce another very ancient danger connected with premarital sex—venereal disease. (Of course venereal disease is not confined to premarital intercourse, but many states require blood tests from couples getting a marriage license so that they can become aware of any venereal disease either of them may have before they marry.)

In an article entitled "Did He Leave You with More Than a Memory?" the author says that there are more than 20 sexually-transmitted diseases. Of these, five must be reported to the Department of Health by your doctor because they are so hazardous to health and are highly contagious. The five are: syphilis, gonorrhea, chancroid, granuloma inquinale, lymphogranuloma.[9]

Three lesser-known sexually transmitted diseases, which do not as yet have to be reported to the Department of Health, are now occurring in epidemic proportions: nongonococcal urethritis, genital herpes, and trichomoniasis.[10]

The American Social Health Association estimated in a 1980 report that from five to twenty million Americans have herpes. The number is growing at the rate of approximately 500,000 cases a year.[11]

So, what's the big flap? If so many people have VD of some sort, it couldn't be all that bad, right? Wrong! For example, nongonococcal urethritis and gonorrhea can both result in pelvic inflammatory disease (PID); approximately 10 percent of the women who get PID the first time become sterile; by the fourth time most women will be sterile.[12]

Genital herpes usually appears in men and women between the ages of 15-30. Herpes is linked to cancer of the cervix which afflicts 16,000 women in the U.S. in its serious form and contributes to 7,400 deaths a year. It can be passed on to newborn babies. Each year several hundred babies are born with herpes simplex; more than half of them die. The survivors often suffer permanent neurological damage.[13]

"The initial outbreak in women is often severe and incapacitating. Numerous sores break out on the external genitals and vagina, and the lymph nodes in the groin become swollen. These ulcers, which may last for weeks, are often accompanied by fever, chills, headache and muscle pain. The virus backs off after a while, but two-thirds of the women who have had it once get it repeatedly. Menstruation can trigger a recurrence. Fever from a cold or other illness can also trigger recurrence."[14] The disease can exist without symptoms in both men and women; therefore, they can give it to each other without knowing it. It can lie dormant until something stirs it up, and researchers are unsure of the number of things that can stir it up.

As you can see, VD seems to be the hardest on girls and women. And this favoritism doesn't stop at venereal disease. There's always pregnancy.

An Associated Press article about unwed mothers said that "nearly one in three white teenagers and more than four out of five black teenagers giving birth in 1979 were not married" (Census Bureau statistics). "This is all happening despite the fact that birth control is more widely available and abortion is more accepted. Among the reasons, experts say, is that more women want to marry at a later age and there is less of a social stigma for an unmarried mother who decides to keep her child."[15]

Although the above reasons appear to be valid, I think the problem still goes back to a situation that exists today in most homes in our country, and that is that many of our teenagers feel alienated and unloved by their families. Going through the turbulent adolescent years with little perceived love or security in their lives, many teenagers essentially *choose* to get pregnant. That is, they feel they need to love something, and more importantly they need something to love them.

The sad truth is that few teenagers are mature enough to take on the great responsibility of raising a child. These teenage girls who feel that they have this great amount of love to share with another human being would be wise to adopt a kitten from a local humane society. All parties concerned would be much better off. The cycle perpetuates itself in a home where the pregnant teenager chooses to keep her own baby. The greatest thing a father and mother can do for a child is to love that child with all their hearts. That's obviously very difficult when there isn't a father in the home. So the cycle gets repeated once again: the young, teenage daughter, with the encouragement of others, keeps her child then pawns the child off on Grandma, literally. Over a period of years

Grandma develops a maternal relationship with a child and not a grandmother role. I've seen young mothers go off to college and chase down bachelor's degrees as well as master's degrees while Grandma is raising the child. It's a wise teenager who has the foresight and courage to give up her child for adoption to a young couple who can't have children of their own. The question has to be asked, Whose needs are being met by keeping the child? Does the mother have her own best interests at heart, or her baby's? Tough decision for a young kid to make.

People Magazine, reporting on information from the Alan Guttmacher Institute, says that almost 90 percent of teenage mothers are deciding to keep their babies, and nearly one-half of the nation's 543,000 illegitimate births are to teenagers. They go on to say that between 1970 and 1978 the number of sexually-active teenagers increased by 50 percent. By the age of 19 only one-fifth of boys and one-third of girls have *not* had intercourse.[16]

Thirty thousand girls 13 to 14 years old conceive each year.[17] These young mothers under 15 are five times more likely to die during childbirth than women 20 to 24. And infant deaths are twice as high among babies born to teenage mothers.[18]

Many of us tend to ignore statistics such as these, until we become one of them. These statistics come from some of the periodicals young people read—*Mademoiselle, Ms., Senior Scholastic*, etc. And high school and college students are taught these facts in their various classes. But they don't hear them until their parents take an interest in their welfare and point out these very prevalent problems to them. Are you brave enough to take the responsibility to open up and share with your son or daughter? Let's face it. It's difficult to talk to anyone about sex. Even more difficult to talk about sex with your son or daughter. Again, because no one ever talked to us, right?

It would be so much easier if we could just slip a brochure under our teenager's door filled with all the facts that we would like them to know. Then just attach a note to the brochure, "If you have any questions at all, please feel free to contact me at my toll-free number at my office." But you see, teenagers need more than just information. What teenagers need is love and understanding, and a commitment on their parents' part to get involved in their lives.

I can't think of a better way to become involved with your teenagers than to share some real life experiences that may not only show your teenagers that you are not really the product of the archaic Dark Ages, but that you do realize the many struggles and temptations they face. When you're brave enough to share some real life experiences from your life, then maybe your teenager *might* be willing to share some of their real thoughts and feelings with you.

If you're wondering about how to get started on something like this, if you haven't had a regular time of getting away with your son or daughter, you might be wise to start right now. Now you're probably thinking, "Wonderful. Sure. My teenager is just going to love to go away with his or her mom or dad." You have to learn to walk before you run. I suggest that you begin to make some inroads in this area. Touch base with the adolescent—take him out for lunch or dinner to the restaurant of his choice. Then after you have made a few attempts—feeble as they might be—to establish intimacy with your son or daughter, plan a family weekend away together or perhaps a weekend with one of your children and yourself.

I know it's difficult to find time for these things, but as most of us as parents are aware, our kids grow up too quickly. I know my own schedule is a tremendously hectic one, yet I've taken my children, one at a time, out of school to business trips with me when I'm conducting a seminar or doing a television program in another city. It's a very unique time that we have together. We have fun and we laugh, but more importantly we have some time just for the two of us, and my children look forward to this very special time. They would literally forsake any of their own activities to hop on an airplane and go with me. We always come back closer and with a better understanding of each other and we both feel like it's well worth it.

If the thought of a heavy conversation with your son or daughter is scary even to think about, start with something light. Have you ever shared some of the crazy, foolish, dumb, weird things you did as a teenager? Kids thoroughly enjoy listening to Mom's and Dad's antics as teenagers. What a great way to show your children—who think you were actually classmates with Tom Edison and Benjamin Franklin—that you truly were a kid at one time.

There is a special relationship in families between moms and sons and between dads and daughters. Think just for a moment about where you got all of your information about sex. Didn't you get it from other misinformed friends? Or from dirty stories or restroom walls? Research tells us that very few people are privileged enough to get a good, honest, open dialogue going with their parents. This is a crime for us who claim to be Christian parents. To not talk about one of God's greatest gifts—sex—in exactly the way God presented it to us, as a gift with specific guidelines for its use, is a tragedy that is relived in many lives today.

Before we stop talking about "Mating" I feel it's important to cover another subject that is becoming more and more of a problem—living together. It used to be called "shacking up" but we've come to accept it as a normal thing so we've dressed up the description.

Kay and John were a typical example of couples I see in my private practice so often today. John is 23, Kay is 22. They lived together for two years and have been married for only about six months. The day after they got married things began to disintegrate. All of a sudden they were confronted with problems that never existed when they were living together. They were legitimately confused and puzzled as they came for marital therapy. I say they're typical because John and Kay and thousands of other couples like them made a judgment error. They really thought that living together was a foolproof way to test whether or not they were compatible for marriage.

You really can't blame them for thinking along those lines. It does seem to make sense, on the surface, that living together might be a good way to really find out if it would work for them. The Census Bureau reports that the number of couples living together has more than doubled since 1970. Nancy Evans, in *Glamour* Magazine, lists several reasons people give for living together.

1. One out of three marriages end in divorce, so why bother?

2. It would be a lie to promise to love somebody forever. People change in the course of their lives, and not necessarily the same way.

3. Why ruin a good thing? Marriage somehow changes relationships for the worse.

4. Marriage is constricting. They don't want to make a commitment. This last reason emphasizes "me" rather than "we" which results in greater expectations from marriages than it did in past generations.[19]

Why is it that so many couples really get along fairly well while they live together but when they get married things don't go half as well? I think the key is commitment—or lack of commitment. Living together is the heaviest form of dating. It isn't the same as a marriage commitment because couples who just live together never entirely take off their masks. They are still on their best behavior, as they are on their dates. They don't become the true people they really are.

Living together is a commitment not to make a commitment. The couple who lives together has an open-ended agreement with each other. In a marriage, however, the commitment is to each other and is made in front of everyone and God, and the consequences of breaking that commitment seem greater. Of course, stakes are much higher in marriage than they are in living together. You really have more to live up to when you become a husband and wife before Almighty God. We live in an age when commitment is looked down upon in many quarters. However, when it comes to that true intimacy that so many young men and women apparently yearn for, it can only be attained through marriage. You can never be one in spirit without being committed to each other and to the Creator of your lives. Furthermore, recent research tells us that the success of a marriage is probably not enhanced one bit by living together before marriage. Living together is certainly not the way to fly, even for practical reasons—such as very little financial protection, no security, no retirement benefits, and a few other legal protections in general. Especially for a woman there's very little security in a live-in relationship.

In addition to the aforementioned practical reasons, perhaps more important to a woman are the emotional scars that remain throughout her lifetime. On the basis of my working with hundreds of couples during the past decade I have come to the conclusion that there are several basic differences in men and women. One of the most obvious to me is the fact that as men we are able to separate the physical and emotional quite easily. I've had men tell me that they've been good husbands and have had only five, six or eight women during their marriage. For whatever reason, men seem to be able to distinguish between physical relationship and emotional relationship more easily than women. The fact remains that women, more so than men, tend to carry the emotional scars of a relationship that doesn't last.

For many women, guilt associated with living together prior to marriage is an added burden that they must carry through life. Even though they intellectualize their living together, and on the surface appear to have rejected their parents' values as well as the religious instruction they received as a child; for some reason they are unable to shake these guilt feelings. Even if they later marry the man with whom they have lived, many of them suffer a great deal of guilt. The guilt is really a two-edged sword that has to be dealt with, whether the guilt is precipitated by violating their own personal standards and values, or whether they violated their parents' values and standards. It really is a rare individual who can reject family values and live a life-style contrary to those values without suffering from guilt.

A couple of times in this book I'm going to share with you a transcript of a session with one of my clients. Chuck gave me permission to share this tape of his life with you because he hopes someone will be helped by his experiences. While we were talking about premarital sex, Chuck said the following:

"Premarital sex is something I would never have dreamed I'd be talking to anyone about because, along with alcohol and dope, as I was going through school, sex was also the thing to do. You weren't cool if you hadn't been laid in a while. I remember how embarrassed I'd be when I told my friends I hadn't been laid by a certain girl I went out with. It just wasn't cool. It wasn't really until I'd grown up a little bit that I found out just what kind of adverse effect premarital sex has. Especially for the woman. I hate to say that; I hate to sound biased, but especially for the woman.

"I have a good friend who shared how she and her boyfriend were both Christians and madly in love with each other. They just knew they were the right ones for each other. They engaged in premarital sex—she gave herself to him literally, because in sex the two really do become one. Premarital sex puts a strain on a relation-ship because the relationship then becomes just physical. Instead of meeting and talking, sharing your day, going to a movie, just enjoying being with each other, you get together, have sex and leave. Just to fulfill your needs, you might say.

"Anyhow, this friend and her boyfriend, after a couple of months, found out that they weren't right for each other, they weren't meant to get married. She's 21 years old, a college graduate and a beautiful girl. As she told me about this I could see in her eyes the hurt she had gone through. She said she would wake up in the morn-ing and vomit blood because she was so upset. She had given herself to somebody and he wasn't the right per-son, and she couldn't get back what she had lost. It's kind of like giving someone a million dollars and later finding out you gave it to the wrong person, but now he's gone and so is your money. Gone for good. You don't have it anymore. And the person who should have had it will now never get it.

"I recently started going out with a girl that I knew a few years ago. One thing I admired back then, really liked and respected about her, was that she wasn't messing around with anybody. Even when I was messing around with drugs and alcohol I still had a high ideal of what I wanted in a girl, and this girl was my kind of woman because she didn't give in to guys. Well, after I became a

Christian, this girl came back into my life. We started going out to dinner and talking and sharing our lives. It was just beautiful. She was just as lovely as she was the day I first met her.

"One day she shared some experiences she was struggling with. She said that she had made love with this guy. She looked at me and said, 'Chuck, if there is some way I could just turn back the hands of time . . .' I don't think this guy was worried about it, but I can guarantee you she was. He had given her the ultimatum that 'if you love me you will,' and she did, so she did. She never felt right about it and it really had a traumatic psychological effect on her.

"Then when we were having dinner one night she told me about another guy. She thought she was going to marry him and lived with him for two years while she went through college. I can't tell you what her telling me that did to me. It was like a slap in the face. Here was this girl I thought was so special, that I had such high regard for, telling me that she lived with somebody for two years. For some reason that just didn't set with me right. I had hoped that the woman I would fall in love with and marry would share all the little deep secrets of her mind, her feelings and her philosophy with just me. I think when you're lying in bed with different people all of the time it's kind of hard to know who's special and who's not. Don't get me wrong. She wasn't laying around with a lot of different people, but living two years with a guy, a lot of things can happen between them.

"But when I talked with Dr. Leman about this he explained to me that I had taken away a lot of those special things from girls I had sex with in high school. That really hit me. Some of those girls know in the back of their minds that they will have to share our experiences with the ones they fall in love with. I can imagine how those boyfriends are going to feel. I feel it once, but I might have caused it 10 times.

"I know one girl who told me she doesn't hold or kiss or anything on a date. By today's standards that's kind of hard to believe. She's not a Mormon or anything like that; she's a beautiful college girl; but she doesn't want to get trapped in any kind of a relationship until she gets married. She wants to keep all her dates on a friendship basis. I think that's neat."

Waiting

As we said before, it seems that teenagers want, all at once, everything life has to offer them. It's hard to wait. But when teenagers rush into a sexual relationship, or marriage, or independence, almost without exception it ends up disastrously.

One tough question for teenagers to deal with is, Should I date non-believers? This is a question for which God's Word does offer some specific advice. In 2 Corinthians 6:14 we read, "Don't be teamed with those who do not love the Lord, for what do the people of God have in common with the people of sin? How can light live with darkness?"

As a marriage and family counselor I deal with the problem of Christians dating non-Christians, or Christian/non-Christian marriages quite frequently. Many young people have, of course, a great amount of ambition and determination. When your daughter finds the right man, even though he may have a few faults, she figures, "Oh, he's going to be different after we're married. He says he'll start going to church (quit drinking, stop running around, get a job)." She is naive enough to think she can change the other person.

If she just loves him enough he'll change is a fallacy to begin with. There's no way that any of us can change another person; not someone we're married to, or a son or daughter or mother or father. All we can do is change our own behavior which might, in the long run—and sometimes that's a real long run—help the other person change his or her behavior. If a teenager is really set on marrying a Christian or a person who has all the qualities he or she is looking for, then it would probably be wise to date only that kind of person.

Cheryl was one of those women who was determined that things would work out. She and Dave were in love; but Dave didn't share Cheryl's faith. After seven years of marriage and steadily growing farther and farther apart in their relationship, and lugging their children back and forth to church without Dave, Cheryl did something that she really wished hadn't happened—she had an affair with a young married man in her church.

The affair lasted about a year and a half before she came to grips with the fact that her lover was never going to leave his wife. She was really trapped. She was trapped in a marriage where she had grown more and more distant from her husband, and now she had gotten herself into an affair that literally tore her up.

Any situation that would create dissidence between a couple and divide them should be avoided. Marrying someone who doesn't believe as you do is asking for troubles. Today Cheryl's still trying to put the pieces together in her original marriage, but she isn't getting much cooperation from Dave. And even though she's absolutely guilt ridden by her affair with the married man, she is still very much in love with him; however, he has shown very little interest in wanting to see her again.

If you have an idea of the kind of person you want to spend your life with, then you'd better look for those qualities in him or her now. Because after you're married there is very little chance that he or she will change. In fact, you might discover that the things you dislike about that person only intensify.

Do you suppose that when a young couple walks down the flower-strewn aisle of the church on their wedding day that they're thinking about getting a divorce in a few years? No, I don't think so, either. But statistics show that the average marriage today lasts just seven years. That's one of the reasons why it's so fundamentally important for us to understand the very temporary nature of early romantic love. Many couples run blindly into relationships that are primarily physical. Physical intimacy in a sense takes the place of a sincere relationship so that young lovers are robbed of the opportunity to really get to know each other. They don't get a chance to talk, communicate or even think, much less share experiences. So they end up getting a very unrealistic view of love and marriage.

Kathy and Ron were married at age 16. Kathy was escaping from an unhealthy situation in her home—her father was abusive to her and she very much needed the comfort and "love" of a male. Ron also had an unhappy home life. His mother was an alcoholic, so he too wanted to run away from something.

So these two people, who had great amounts of insecurity, were literally forced together in love. Unfortunately, the love was not a lasting love but a physical love, a love that went by the wayside very soon after they were married. Kathy had two children by Ron and, by the time she was 19, she was divorced with two young children.

These young people made a mistake in judgment that could have been avoided. Kathy and Ron both had poor self-concepts. Because they were insecure they sought out people who would give them comfort and fill that void in their lives. Unfortunately for that insecure young couple, when things got rough after they were married and they really needed to communicate with each other and rely on something other than their physical relationship, they had nothing. Absolutely nothing. There was no choice but to go their separate ways.

There's no point in continuing in a life-style that's full of mistakes and wrong decisions. We all make judgment errors and do foolish things. We can learn from our mistakes. We as parents need to try to impart this to our children. The only way we can is to share our own mistakes. Sometimes it's very difficult to share our weaknesses with them. But when we do share our weaknesses with our children, that really gives them strength and encouragement, perhaps, to be open and honest with us.

I think of my own two daughters who one night were with me at a softball game. I'm a fast-pitch pitcher in a city recreation league. It was the first inning and I wasn't even in the ball game. I was simply coaching first base because the other pitcher was on the mound that evening. Well, in the first inning the umpire made an unbelievably poor call on a high pitch and I yelled out, "You're crazy," and the umpire jumped out from behind the plate, took off his mask and shouted down the first base line, "What did you say?" And I said, "You're crazy." He said, "You're out of the ball game." And I retorted, "Well, I'm out of the ball game but you're still crazy."

The rules call for players to leave not only the field but the entire park when they're thrown out of the ball game. Well, needless to say, I was embarrassed. It was honestly the first time I had ever been thrown out of a ball game of any kind and I wasn't even playing. Well, my two young daughters were with me and they were just getting a good hard play on the swings and slides and rings in the park, and I called to them, "Come on girls, we've got to go home."

They looked at me rather astonished and said,

"Home! We just got here. Why're we going home?"

I said, "Come on, get ready to go home. Get in the car, hurry." They reluctantly went along and began to press me for a reason when we got to the car. Well, I found myself about to lie to my children. Tell them some kind of fish story, but I caught myself. I turned to my younger daughter Krissy and said, "Krissy, what happens when you talk back to Daddy?"

She looked at me real puzzled and said, "We get sent to our room?"

And I said, "Yeah, that's right. Daddy just talked back to the umpire, and the umpire sent Daddy to his room." My children understood that one real good. So good that the first thing they blurted out as we entered our home several minutes later was, "Mommy, Mommy, guess what? Daddy got kicked out of the ball game." So the lesson is, when *we* make mistakes, our kids can learn from them.

Chapter 4

Getting, Scoring and Conquering

One night, not long after my second book, *Sex Begins in the Kitchen*, was published, I was tucking in my nine-year-old daughter, Holly. As we had on previous occasions, we spent some time talking about sex. I think Holly had a pretty good notion of what sex was all about, but I really wanted to talk with her rather matter-of-factly about the nitty-gritty of intercourse. I explained that intercourse took place when Daddy put his penis into Mommy's vagina. No sooner had I gotten those words out of my mouth than Holly looked up at me and exclaimed, "How gross!"

Well, I must admit I laughed out loud. But how else would a nine-year-old girl think about intercourse? Although nine-year-olds aren't generally overtly interested in the opposite sex, my experience has shown that nine-, ten- and eleven-year-old children spend a great deal of time thinking about the opposite sex, and about sex as well. It's a shock to many of us as parents, who are used to having our little girls and boys climb up on our laps, to discover that suddenly they become all grown up.

Do you remember the time you walked into the bathroom when your 13-year-old was in there? The chewing out you got probably rivaled that of an army private at boot camp. Children are rarely subtle when they let us parents know that things are changing in their lives and that they're quickly hurtling themselves toward the world of adolescence.

Let's Talk About Sex—Now!

It might be hard for some of us parents to realize that our teenagers will, by the time their seventeenth birthdays roll around, have ample opportunities to have sex. And the statistics of teenagers' sexual activity are disturbing, to say the least: 80 percent of boys and 67 percent of girls under 19 have experienced intercourse.[20]

Of the some 21,000,000 adolescents in the U.S. between the ages of 15 and 19, 11,000,000 are estimated to have had sexual intercourse at least once. And of the 8,000,000 13- to 14-year-olds, 1.5 million are estimated to have had intercourse at least once. Approximately 30,000 girls ages 13 to 14 conceive each year.[21]

Now these statistics are enough to scare many of us parents into some kind of action. But what is disturbing about this whole thing is the fact the teenagers are ignorant to the realities of sex. Authorities—counselors, physicians, pastors—point out repeatedly that teenagers have many misconceptions about sex: sex at mid-cycle is safe; conception can't occur the first time they have sex; coitus interruptus is safe; etc.

When you think of sex, what do you think of? Something nobody should talk about? Something shady or forbidden? Or do you think about something that's really neat, wonderful, priceless and truly a gift? I hope you think about it as a gift, because that's what it is. It's really a gift from God. In fact, sex was God's idea first. And He planned it, it wasn't simply an afterthought He had. God created us as sexual beings and the Scripture says that God looked upon everything He created as "excellent in every way" (Gen. 1:31). That includes our sexual abilities.

Think about the time you, as a husband or wife, had perhaps the greatest sexual experience of your married life. You ought to be smiling now. Are you? Where did that ability to reach that pulsating orgasm come from? Where did those special feelings come from? Those are really God-given feelings.

We have the capacity to be sexual in the truest sense of the word even at birth. Studies indicate, for example, that male infants still in their mother's womb have erections. Kids at a very early age discover the pleasure of self-stimulation of the genital area. So God created us in such a way that we can experience these feelings right from the very beginning. These are natural feelings, not dirty, nasty or "down there." Then how did most of us adults, and adolescents as well, get such a negative perception of sex?

One reason is that parents aren't able to talk with their children about sex. We find it very, very uncomfortable. And, of course, we parents are uncomfortable because our parents never talked to us about sex. As a psychologist it's necessary for me to talk to people about their sex lives. I do that routinely with almost everyone I see. When I first began private counseling and had to ask the question, "How's your sex life?" I'm here to tell you that it made me very uncomfortable. It was something, like everything else, that I had to learn to do.

Our kids usually hear very little from us parents about one of the most important forces in our lives—our sexuality. We neglect to counsel, warn and advise them about the use or misuse of this important gift from God. As a matter of fact, most teenage girls find out whether or not they are pregnant without any assistance from their parents. Parents need to keep communication lines open with their teenagers on the subject of sex as well as other areas.

There's Only One Right Way

Darrell Royal, former University of Texas head football coach, once said that there were three things that could happen when you made a forward pass, and two of them were bad. So it is with sex.

Sex is for married couples, between husband and wife only. These seem like hard words, especially in light of today's values. Yet there are many reasons, besides the biblical ones, why teenagers should avoid becoming sexual athletes. But every Monday morning, in every locker room on every high school or college campus, you hear guys asking each other, "Did you score Friday night? What did you get?" And you know what they're talking about. There seems to be some kind of a contest to see who can conquer the most girls the fastest.

It's hard to figure out why two 15-year-old girls would have a race to see who could lose her virginity first. This was the case of one of my young clients and her girl friend. It's hard to believe that they would want to have sex that first time when research strongly suggests that a woman's first sexual experience is not a satisfying one. Katherine Bement Davis told of one study with 1,000 educated married women. The study found that one-fourth of them were repelled by their first sexual experience.[22] There seems to be similar agreement along that line in many other studies. Paul Popenoe, director of American Institute of Family Relations, found that in a survey of 658 women only 25 percent of them achieved a normal climax at first intercourse. Only seven percent achieved climax in the first 30 days, an additional 26 percent between one and eleven months, 16 percent one year or more. Six percent reported never being able to attain a normal orgasm.[23]

My 15-year-old client reported to me that her first sexual experience "hurt like hell," and her date was very drunk, left her in the park and drove himself home. In many circles of young people today it really is a cool thing to lose your virginity, the earlier the better. She won the race alright, but what a price she had to pay.

One of my observations about people is this: they want what they can't have. A teenage girl who refuses to let her body be used, who doesn't follow the crowd in the sexual contests but seems to be a little different from everyone else, is a cut above all the rest. She truly is someone who is worth dating, pursuing, admiring and caring for.

Sex is a gift, and teenagers can accept that gift. That's the easy part. The hard part is to make wise decisions concerning its use. The key is to keep themselves out of situations where they are used or abused in any way, shape or form. People are for loving; things are for using. Don't use others, and don't let someone else use you. There will always be some jerk who will gladly use you for his own satisfaction. Whether that jerk be a young man or a young woman, there're plenty of them around. The neat thing is that we really do have true liberty as Christians. God gives us the absolute freedom to decide for ourselves how we're going to conduct ourselves. But as the Fram Oil Filter man tells us, we can pay now or pay later. We can follow the rules and enjoy life to the maximum or abuse God's gifts and pay for it the rest of our lives. It's our decision.

I think Christians sometimes feel they aren't really free to decide, that God is going to push things down their throats. I haven't found that indicated in the Scripture. All the Scriptures I have read tell me that God always lets us choose the way we go. He never forces Himself or His will on us in any way. We are created with freedom of will, we can accept Him and His teachings or reject Him.

I think of Revelation 3:20, "I have been standing at the door and I am constantly knocking. If anyone hears me calling him and opens the door, I will come in and fellowship with him and he with me." I love that painting of Jesus knocking at the door; there's no doorknob on His side of the door. We have to open the door from the inside—from our hearts; we have to invite even Almighty God into our lives by way of Jesus Christ. That's how much God loves us, even to the extent of letting us make the decision to open the door to Him or reject Him.

So, what are some of the reasons why you should decide not to have sex before you are married?

It's Alright to Say, "I Don't Want To"

Many teenagers know they aren't ready for sex yet. "I don't want to" is a pretty good reason not to have sex. It's the only reason you really need. If you find yourself doing things in life that you really don't want to do you're going to, sooner or later, become very confused, angry and resentful. You need to reaffirm your right to say no. (Many of us had our early inclinations to say no beaten out of us by parents who insisted that children didn't have the right to say no.)

Traditionally many a girl has told herself, "I gave myself to him. He said if I loved him I would prove it to him." In the 1980s women can no longer blame men. All of us are responsible for our own actions. Young women who allow other people to control their emotions, that is, tell them what to do with their bodies, end up being very unhappy women someday with husbands who tell them what to do and how to do it.

One thing is clear, each of us is responsible for our own actions, and each of us needs to work on being in control of our emotions rather than having our emotions control us. But, you ask, aren't young men and women going to get together in some way, shape or form? Of course, they are. Like a moth to a flame young men and young women will find each other. Where we fail as parents is that we issue essentially an ultimatum to our teenagers to not do anything. Now that's unrealistic. When young men and young women get together there's going to be some kind of physical activity. But it's the wise teenager who knows that he or she must set limits. But we keep coming back to: Yes, but where do we draw the line? Hold hands? Kiss a little bit? Make out a lot? Pet just a little bit? Or heavy petting? Just how far does one go?

First of all, I think it's unrealistic to think that a teenager should have the same limit for all situations. For example, there might be a young man that a young woman is not interested in even vaguely; she may not even want to hold his hand or show any kind of encouragement to him on her first date. By mentally setting an all-inclusive limit she is creating a bad situation. Nobody should feel like she has to hold hands with some jerk she's not interested in.

Teenagers have a tremendously high need to be wanted, but most of them do not really want a heavy sexual relationship. They only submit out of fear of being rejected. But if somebody really cares for you and loves you, they're not going to demand their own way. That is really counter to what love is. And the one who demands or tempts you to have a sexual relationship is in big trouble. Listen to what Jesus told His disciples in Luke 17: "There will always be temptations to sin,. . . but woe to the man [or woman] who does the tempting. If he were thrown into the sea with a huge rock tied to his neck, he would be far better off than facing the punishment in store for those who harm these little children's souls. I am warning you!" (vv. 1-3).

There doesn't seem to be a lot of room for argument on that one. If you're tempting someone else, then you'd better be ready to face the punishment of the Almighty. So each of us really has the right to say no. And we all—adults and children—need practice in saying no; it's okay to say no. You don't have to do what everybody else wants you to do.

The ability to say no is one of the skills I had to learn in my life, and I'm still learning it. I get hundreds of invitations to speak during a given year. I really had to master the skill of saying, "No, I can't do it. Sorry. Glad to help you but that would really interfere with my time with my wife and family." Like all other skills it takes practice to say no. The teenager today, facing the turbulent world of adolescence, is going to have plenty of opportunities when he or she should say no. There's a sea full of people out there who are ready, willing and quite able to use you for their own hedonistic satisfaction.

I used to run around with a guy in high school who even went to the extreme of having notches on his belt. Let your mind wander at this point and guess what those notches represented—conquests, scores. What a terrible way to look at something as special as sex.

Girls, do you want to be represented as a notch in some vacuous guy's belt?

Pregnancy Is a Pretty Good Reason to Say No

The second reason for saying no to sex is to avoid unwanted pregnancies—either your own or, if you're a boy, your girl friend's. The statistics are appalling. Every year more than one million teenage girls get pregnant. Thirty thousand of them are under 15 years of age.[23] Nearly one-half of the nation's 543,000 illegitimate births are to teenagers. If the present trend continues, four out of every ten young women will have at least one pregnancy while still in her teens.[24]

The threat of pregnancy is an excellent reason to say no, isn't it? Most of our teenagers are at the highest level of sexual drive that they'll have in their lives. This fact, accompanied by the ignorance most adolescents have about sex, contraception and basic facts of life, creates a tremendously explosive and tragic situation. Even if pregnancy is terminated by abortion, many times the experience is the final chapter in a relationship between a young man and a young woman.

As human beings we have a way of telling ourselves that things that are unhappy or unpleasant won't happen to us. I recently had the misfortune of having my wallet stolen from my hotel room when I was on the road. The funny thing was that I remember wondering about leaving the wallet in the room. I even checked the lock on the door to see if it was a substantial lock and made a conscious decision to leave the wallet there. I guess I told myself that this isn't my standard procedure. "It's just once, and nothing will happen." Well, it happened. A thief came into my room, used both of my credit cards and put $3,300 worth of charges on one card and $3,500 on the other.

Many a teenager plays Russian roulette with sex. I don't know if it's a subconscious way of dealing with their basic desires to bear a child or if it's just a lie that they tell themselves to allow them to enjoy something that basically isn't very good for them. But, simple as it sounds, ask any teenager who has turned up pregnant and most likely she will tell you that she really never thought that it could happen to her. She may have thought that she was too young to conceive. Or perhaps she held the misconception that, on first sex, she couldn't conceive. Infatuated teenagers are somehow oblivious to the realities of life.

Remember that special day when your firstborn came into the world? Perhaps the new mother was lucky enough to have her husband with her. What a special day to see that little life come into the world. I know when my firstborn came into our lives I marveled at the majesty of it all. I remember looking through the glass of the nursery and thinking that she was the most beautiful baby in the entire nursery. And as I watched her, tears filled my eyes and streamed down my face. Tears of joy, admiration, an overwhelming feeling of how special that little life truly is.

I think in contrast to Amy, age 16, who after four counseling sessions broke the news to me that she was pregnant. I think she needed some time to feel me out and see if I was worthy of sharing this secret she had shared with no one. A child giving birth to a child. Amy was going to do it all without letting her parents in on it. She had things all worked out. She and her boyfriend were going to be married. It was really special because Gary loved her and she loved Gary. I had the feeling that Amy didn't really believe what she was saying, but she did a pretty good job of trying to convince herself as she tried to convince me.

It was no surprise to me, and perhaps no surprise to Amy, that Gary suddenly got interested in a private school on the east coast and disappeared from the community without even saying good-bye to her. He literally left her holding the bag. Did that deter Amy? Not one bit. Amy decided that she would keep the baby. She and the baby were going to have a great life together. Research tells us that Amy is very much in line with what other teenage mothers do. Almost 90 percent of teenage mothers today are deciding to keep their babies.[25]

Life isn't easy for Amy these days. I ran into her a couple of years later in a restaurant where she was bussing tables. She worked the lunch and dinner hours and then hustled off to her one night school course. She told me that it was very difficult for her to get to class on time because many times she had to stay over and work late. In our short conversation I learned that Amy's 54-year-old mom was caring for her child. I was left with the impression that the child was really more her mom's than Amy's.

My concern is not only for Amy but for her little daughter. I'm wondering, without a father in the home, how Amy's daughter is going to learn about men. And I'm wondering if there's ever going to be a time in Amy's life when she finds a special man to love her and her little daughter. I certainly hope so, but realistically, even at the tender age of 18, Amy has two strikes against her, and so does her daughter.

The possibility of an unwanted pregnancy is a very good reason for saying no to sex before marriage.

Trapped in an Unwanted Marriage

A third reason for saying no is that an unwanted marriage might be thwarted. I've personally met older couples who have been married many years, but never really loved each other and were actually trapped because they felt they had to get married because she was pregnant. Some couples, even when pregnancy isn't a factor, deceive themselves into thinking that they love each other, or more often, are driven to marriage by guilt feelings because of their sexual experience with each other. I know that might seem crazy in this day and age, but as we continually see, guilt takes its toll on people of all ages. It's the smart person who avoids situations in his or her life where the guilties are not going to do a number on them.

In this day of contraceptives and abortion you'd think such a thing would be rare. I've never taken a survey of the number of my clients who have had abortions, but the percentage is extremely high. However, the anti-abortion group is very large. Many people do not believe in terminating a pregnancy by abortion. So, of course, the alternative is to have the baby.

Thousands of families can't handle illegitimate births, so thousands of teenagers face "shotgun weddings."

I recently worked with a 28-year-old woman and her 29-year-old husband, Randy. I started out seeing them together because they were complaining of marital diffi-culties. But as our therapy progressed it became evident that Debbie was very depressed. I told Randy I wanted to spend several sessions with Debbie alone.

Debbie and Randy were brought up in rather strict homes. Both of them happened to be Catholics. Debbie attended a parochial school and Randy a public school throughout their first 12 school years. By the time I saw them they had been married about 10 years. They loved each other but things just weren't right. Debbie and Randy had a 10-year-old son, Greg. Greg got along beautifully with his father, but terribly with his mother. This was part of the problem with Debbie and Randy's marriage.

After about our third session together I asked Debbie what I had a hunch was really the big question. "Debbie, were you pregnant when you married Randy?" I'll never forget Debbie weeping in my office as she shared with me that she had been pregnant and she felt they had to get married. The pressure she sensed from her own family told her that.

They were married when Debbie was just three months pregnant and she resented that she had to get married. But Debbie and Randy never talked about "having to get married" after they walked down the aisle. She finally divulged her private thoughts to me that, for the past 10 years, she really thought Randy married her only because he had to.

What a joy it was to work with Debbie and Randy and to open up some avenues of communication between them. As it turned out, they loved each other very, very much and they would have married regardless of Greg's impending birth. Debbie's being pregnant at 18 and Randy having to go to work in a bottling company at 19 was no piece of cake. Randy today, at 29, is just finishing his college education. It's been a very tough road for them because Debbie got pregnant. Life has a way of holding us accountable for our decisions.

Debbie and Randy had to get married. It so happened that they really loved each other and now, after some counseling, they are on their way to having a happy marriage. But thousands of couples who didn't love each other "had" to get married. Their hopes of finding someone to love were dashed by making a wrong decision, the decision to have sex before marriage.

That Ages-Old Curse Is Still Around

Another reason to say no to sex before you are married is because of the reality and threat of venereal disease. (We discussed venereal diseases in the previous chapter.) Many venereal diseases do not readily respond to medication and can cause a lot of grief before they are brought under control.

Quite some time ago I worked with a couple who was going through the trauma of discovering that each of them suffered from a venereal disease which led to Julie's having her ovaries removed. Julie and Mort had dreamed of having a family. And Mort's mom and dad were very anxious for grandchildren. Mort was the only son of a very traditional Jewish family. He and Julie had to deal with a lot of overwhelming agony and remorse during their time of counseling. I can't remember ever feeling as empathetic toward a young couple.

Before Julie's operation their life appeared to be so bright, with so many promising things in the future. But the one thing they both wanted the most was now prevented. They were unable to have children of their own. I wonder what Mort and Julie's advice would be toward the young people who, like the majority of teenagers in our country, are considering being sexually active.

What About "Flashbacks"?

Another reason for saying no to sex before marriage is "flashbacks." We live in a time when teenagers are very blasé on the subject of sex. Young men and women go from one casual relationship to another. Having worked on a college campus for several years, I'd watch young coeds come on campus and, two weeks into the semester, see them move out of the dorm and in with their special friend of the opposite sex. At the conclusion of the school year they would break up and return home for the summer job. In the fall they would either live together again or find a new partner. The casualness of these relationships is alarming when you see the high stakes our young people are playing with. I'm wondering if the time is going to come in their lives when they wish there weren't six or eight or many more sexual partners in their background.

Ann, age 33, came to me on referral of her gynecologist. She and Michael were married when she was 26. He walked into her life after Ann graduated from college and was just what she always wanted in a man. During their seven-year-marriage she had positive sexual feelings and was able to reach orgasms only when she fantasized about someone else while having sex with her husband. That was disturbing enough to Ann, but what really got her down were the times she wanted to be close to her husband because he was such a special person. He was a good father to their two children, had a good job, was attentive; he was a good husband all the way around. Because of all these plus qualities in her husband, Ann became more and more distressed with her "flashbacks." She asked her doctor to refer her to a psychiatrist or psychologist. She had to find a way of dealing with the problem.

She told me that when she made love with her husband, as she looked into his eyes and felt his arms around her, the thought of one of her previous lovers would pop into her mind. She said, "As I look into my husband's eyes, I see Jack or Ron or even Steve. I didn't even like Steve, it was a terrible relationship. But the thought of these men is affecting my desire for my husband. And now Michael and I are having tremendous sexual problems in our marriage."

Ann's many sexual lovers were taking a tremendous toll on her marriage to the only man she really loved. So, although it has become vogue to throw out the old-fashioned tradition that a girl should remain a virgin until she marries, there certainly are many practical reasons for abstaining until marriage. Flashbacks, although not one of the reasons typically listed for saying no, is one that's worthy of consideration.

God Says Not To

You might be thinking at this point, "Okay, why should a 17-year-old girl, going with a young man, abstain from sex? They are both virgins, so VD isn't a valid reason. Her boyfriend says he'll take the responsibility of birth control, so pregnancy isn't a concern either. Since they're both virgins, they won't have flashbacks of other lovers if they marry." That brings us to another reason.

It's not only flashbacks that cause guilt feelings. I find in my practice that sometimes—not just months or days after premarital sex—even years later, the guilties are still doing a number on a young man or a young woman. The emotional impact of guilt continues to gnaw incessantly away at a person. Some couples have reported the lack of enjoyment in sex after they marry even though they had a fulfilling sex life prior to marriage. But guilt as a result of premarital sex prevents these couples from experiencing full sexual enjoyment in their marriages.

The guilt feelings come about because they have broken their own moral standards or their family's moral standards. If they have never really grown up and faced family values and made legitimate decisions to reject family values, then these values are still with the child, even if the "child" is a grown adult.

But the question remains, what do you tell teenagers about how to get out of compromising situations? It's great to have six or seven intellectual reasons why one should not engage in premarital sex. But intellectual reasoning might be a little difficult to handle for a 15- 16- or 17-year-old kid who is just about at the very height of his sexual drive, while he is with his girl in the back seat of an automobile or in a dark room. How can we as parents help our kids in this vital area?

I think we can help them to form standards of their own. Acknowledge that the standards they form might be different from yours; however, they very well may end up the same as yours. It's important to grant teenagers the right and the freedom to make those decisions concerning themselves. Being alone with a girl or boyfriend is obviously a time when they are on their own. They should realize that if they break their own standards, they're going to feel guilty about it. Also acknowledge to them that there are going to be times they wished they could indulge; they're going to be tempted and the temptations are very natural. But the question is, are your teenagers going to allow their emotions to control their behavior or are they going to consciously control their emotions? For your Christian son or daughter, once they've made that decision to follow Christ, if they violate God's laws, their conscience is going to bother them.

I personally believe that conscience—that tugging on us telling us that something is wrong—is really the Holy Spirit working in our lives to convict us of our own doing. Romans 9:1 teaches us that the conscience is a tool of the Holy Spirit and is often enlightened by Him. That brings us to our next point.

The final reason for us to say no to sex before marriage (or sex with other than our husband or wife), particularly for us Christians, is that God's Word tells us in many places to do just that—say no. He tells us many times to remain pure and give ourselves only to our husbands or wives. The great gift of sex is supposed to be enjoyed in every sense of the word. But, like most gifts or privileges, sex is accompanied by directions for use and by restrictions and responsibility. Listen to what Paul tells us: "Now your sins are washed away, and you are set apart for God, and he has accepted you because of what the Lord Jesus Christ and the Spirit of our God have done for you. . . . Sexual sin is never right: our bodies were not made for that, but for the Lord, and the Lord wants to fill our bodies with himself. . . . That is why I say to run from sex sin. No other sin affects the body as this one does. When you sin this sin it is against your own body. Haven't you yet learned that your body is the home of the Holy Spirit God gave you, and that he lives within you?" (1 Cor. 6:11,13,18,19).

When we don't act responsibly, if we abuse the gift of sex by treating it with a so-what attitude, someone's going to end up paying for it. Unfortunately for women, they seem to get the dirty end of the deal more so than men. Let's face it, women bear the children and are often saddled with the responsibilities of both motherhood and fatherhood while more often than not the man gets off scot-free.

"Let me add this, dear brothers: You already know how to please God in your daily living, for you know the commands we gave you from the Lord Jesus himself. Now we beg you—yes, we demand of you in the name of the Lord Jesus—that you live more and more closely to that ideal. For God wants you to be holy and pure, and to keep clear of all sexual sin so that each of you will marry in holiness and honor—not in lustful passion as the heathen do, in their ignorance of God and his ways" (1 Thess. 4:1-5). "Let there be no sex sin, impurity or greed among you. Let no one be able to accuse you of any such things. Dirty stories, foul talk and coarse jokes— these are not for you. Instead, remind each other of God's goodness and be thankful. . . . Don't be fooled by those who try to excuse these sins, for the terrible wrath of God is upon all those who do them. Don't even associ- ate with such people. For though once your heart was full of darkness, now it is full of light from the Lord, and your behavior should show it! Because of this light within you, you should do only what is good and right and true" (Eph. 5:3-9).

One evening I was addressing the local chapter of The Fellowship of Christian Athletes on the topic they

asked me to speak on, sex. I supported what I said with
God's Word and told them as best I could from my experience of working with young people that, although it was
very difficult, it was best to abstain from sex until they
were married. Well, I must admit I felt as if I was talking to
a brick wall. I didn't sense much support. I was sinking
fast and I was about to run out of words and throw in the
towel when I saw a hand go up in the back of the room.

In front of about 60 fellow athletes this young man
got up and said, "You guys know Sherry and me. You
know that we've been going together for almost three
years. I want to share something with you that Dr. Leman
just said that really hit me right between the eyes. Six
months ago Sherry and I made a commitment, or recom-
mitment I should say. We were very active sexually. We
love each other very much and, as you know, we're
planning a summer wedding."

About this time I knew something was coming that
was going to be good, powerful, and I was all ears, just
sitting back like the rest of the guys, listening. You
could've heard a pin drop as Dave went on to say that he
and Sherry made the decision six months before to quit
having sex. He said, "I want to share with you guys that
our level of *intimacy* has gone up 100 percent since we
stopped having sex. We recommitted our lives to God,
asking Him to give us the courage to abstain. We realize
that the desires we have for each other are natural, that
they are God given; but if we are really going to glorify
God in our lives we must obey God's laws."

Oh, I tell you, that young man set if off. I didn't have
to say another word. I concluded my talk at that moment
and went to an informal time of sharing and answering
questions. What a joy it was to see that young man get to
his feet and share. I'm sure it wasn't easy for him to get
up and expose the intimacies of his life with his fiancée in

front of 60 athletes; but he did, and that makes the difference.

"God's laws are perfect"; when we obey them "they protect us, make us wise, and give us joy and light. . . . God's laws are pure, eternal, just"; they will never become old fashioned (Ps. 19:7-9).

Chapter 5

Love, a Four-Letter Word?

Parents, do you remember when you fell in love? There's not a feeling like it in all the world. Now let's see, the first six times I fell in love, some of the things I remember are the excitement of getting a girl friend, the thrill of giving her a friendship ring, and the disappointment at learning that the dummy left it in her jeans' pocket and it got totaled in the wringer washing machine.

I guess I did fall in love six or seven times, and each time seemed a little more wonderful than the first. But of course the love I'm talking about is what we commonly refer to as *puppy love*. Everybody falls in puppy love. Even parents did at one time. So here again is an opportunity to dig into your memory bank and tell your children some of the happy moments you had during your puppy love experiences in your adolescent years.

I think it really helps if we can tell kids, prior to their adolescence, that they are probably going to experience some of the same things we did. Somebody is going to come into their lives who is so special they can't wait till morning to see him or her again at school. Puppy love makes young men all of a sudden become compulsive about brushing their teeth and combing their hair, and sneaking a little bit of Dad's after-shave. Or it makes a young girl stand in front of a mirror trying out special smiles, practicing looking cool and disinterested, or combing her hair into perfection so Mr. Right will think it's naturally that way.

What is love? How do we know the difference between infatuation and real love? I remember the day I met my wife. Of course, our meeting was more memorable than most because, as I already told you, I met her in the men's room at the Tucson Medical Center in Arizona. I was a janitor and she was a nurse's aide. I knew there was something special about her from the very beginning. I had seen her on a couple of occasions around the hospital and on a few occasions she had said hello to me; but I could never quite muster up any response other than "good morning." By the time our eyes met that fateful day in the men's room she was probably beginning to wonder if I was in fact a little weird. Maybe I'd better explain.

I was a janitor and I was cleaning the men's room. You know how the janitor puts one of those mobile trash barrels in the lavatory doorway to let everyone know he's in there working? Well, I was just emptying some trash into the barrel at the door when my wife-to-be came around the corner. Our eyes met and I blurted out, "Do you want to go to the World's Fair with me?" (Of course, the World's Fair was in Seattle that year.)

She stopped in her tracks and said, "Pardon me?"

That's how we got going. I invited her to go out for a hamburger and, with God as my judge, I ordered one McDonald's cheeseburger and cut it in half with a plastic fork. I couldn't even finish my half, my stomach was so nervous. I shook inside just looking at that woman. She was that special. That was about 19 years ago and it's really been a very special relationship. The first few days, weeks and even months were a great time of infatuation.

We both laugh at the fact that, on our first date, I couldn't get half a cheeseburger down because my stomach was churning so over this woman. If you visited my home and watched me eat now, after being married for over 15 years, we can prove that infatuation doesn't last. That warm, glowing feeling isn't always there. But infatuation can turn into real love as every day, week or month we get to know each other intricately well. Our initial infatuation with each other grew into a steady, loving relationship with which we're both very happy. But that love grew to that point only by the process of sharing and giving, not through taking. I don't really consider myself "lucky" to have Bucky in my life. Although I love her as friend and mother of our children, I really feel that I have received a special gift from God in the form of my wife. I feel that I've worked at nurturing and protecting and cultivating that very special gift.

What Is Love?

People have been trying to define love for centuries. A very famous chapter in the Bible, the Love Chapter, describes how we can know we're in love. When Paul, the author of 1 Corinthians 13, describes the criteria for true love he starts out with two things that love always *is*—patient and kind. Then he lists several things that love *never is*—jealous, envious, boastful, proud, haughty, selfish, rude. Then he follows through with what love *does not do*—demand its own way, act irritable or touchy, hold grudges or notice others' mistakes. He ends his description with what love *does*—rejoices when truth wins, is loyal no matter what and always believes in, expects the best of, and defends the one who is loved.

Love is patient. One thing that dating does for young people, if they approach dating with the right attitude, is give their relationship a test of time. Time is something many of us, especially young people, have a great deal of difficulty with because we want instant gratification. We live in a time of instant everything—from instant Jello, to soup, to TV dinners. So why not instant intimacy with dating? Why not? Because love is *patient.* Love needs time to get to know the other person. Are you good at waiting? True love can wait until marriage for physical intimacy. Any guy who tells a girl that she can prove her love by having sex with him doesn't know what true love is. Love is patient.

Love is kind. Are you kind enough to recognize that these differences you see in your mate are assets in your relationship and not liabilities? Do you focus on the positives in your relationship and minimize the negatives? Do you try to encourage each other in all things? Do you take the time to say, "Thank you, you were sweet to do this"; "I appreciate your saying that"? Do you try to think of nice things to do for your girl friend or boyfriend? If you begin the habit of being kind before you are married, chances are you will continue to be kind to your mate after you're married. Kindness is essential to a good relationship.

Love is never jealous, envious, boastful, proud, haughty, selfish or rude. Do you feel threatened when someone is around your boyfriend or your mate? When a person of the opposite sex talks to your mate do you get a little sick feeling in the pit of your stomach? That's jealousy. True love trusts the other and is not jealous.

Are you truly glad for your friend or your mate when he or she accomplishes something or gets some kind of recognition. If she gets better grades or a better-paying job or makes the dean's list do you feel envious? Or maybe you're the one who gets good grades, has the best job or makes the dean's list. Did you boast about it to your true love? Were you unduly proud or haughty?

Do you listen to your mate, or is your goal in life just to have your mate or your friend listen to you? Communication is really a two-way street, never a one-way filibuster. A person who demands all the attention is usually the one who is boastful or proud.

Do you treat each other with respect? Do you give in to the other's desires and wishes? Do you have a relationship that's built upon respect? Do you ever resort to language that is unbecoming or vulgar? What about name-calling? These actions fall in the categories of selfishness and rudeness.

Love does not demand its own way, act irritable or touchy, hold grudges or pay particular attention to the other's wrongdoing. Love never "gets back" at the other or tries to "get even." Love never demands its own way. I think if I could pick one part of the Love Chapter to measure all relationships with it would be this one: Love does not demand its own way. The other person's feelings are more important. How do you stack up here with your friend or your mate?

Love is not irritable or touchy. Do you admit that sometimes it's the little things about your mate or your friend that drive you up the wall? Do you and your date argue over stupid things? Are really big arguments touched off over little things?

Love doesn't hold grudges or notice the other's mistakes. Are you a bone digger? Are you good at looking back into the past and finding a fault and throwing it up to your loved one? How good are you at asking for forgiveness? At forgiving? Remember God said, "If you don't forgive others, I won't forgive you" (see Matt. 6:15).

*Love always rejoices when truth wins, is loyal no mat-
ter what and always believes in and expects the best of
and defends the one who is loved.* A relationship that is
not built on truth will never be a lasting relationship. A life
built on anything other than total honesty is probably
going to have all kinds of difficulties before it. If you really
love someone you will be loyal to that one no matter
what the cost. You'll always believe in him, always expect
the best of him and always stand your ground in defend-
ing him.

What does all this mean? It means that love goes on
forever, and perhaps the most critical test a relationship
will endure is the test of time. God is the one to look to
when we want to see an example of love. In the beginning of time God looked forward to you and to me and
loved us so much that He made provisions for us to par-
take of His great love—He sent His only Son to die so
that we could live forever in His love. Then He promised
us that nothing could ever happen that would make His
love invalid—not death nor life, nor angels; neither will all
the powers of hell, or our fears or worries; not "where we
are—high above the sky, or in the deepest ocean—nothing will ever be able to separate us from the love of God"
when that love is through Christ.[26]

I don't know how many times people have come to
me for marital therapy and have said, "We fell in love."
Yeah, they fell in love all right; and in the process they hit
their heads and forgot what love is really like. They don't
treat each other like they love each other. They don't do
kind things for each other. They don't put the other's feelings first, they put their own feelings first.

The authors of several books have talked about the
stages of love. They usually list them as: (1) romantic
love, (2) friendship love, (3) agape love. A relationship
between a man and a woman that is true love really

requires all three, not just one or two.

Romantic love is that sensual, sexual kind of love. It is really revelling in the newness of a marital relationship. What a special time this first stage of love is. But if a couple never gets past this first stage, if their relationship is based solely upon the physical relationship, they're in trouble. Because when the tough times come along, their relationship is going to come up short.

Friendship love needs to be developed. Are you and your chosen one really very best friends? Can you talk to each other about everything? Do you enjoy being together? If you found out that you didn't have much time to live on this earth, if you only had a few days left, would you want to spend those last days with that one you've given yourself to?

The third level is the level that couples need to continually strive for—*agape* love. Agape love is sacrificial love. Agape is the love that helps you put the other's feelings first. Agape love is not found on the first date, or the first year, or maybe even the first five years of a relationship. It has to be developed and nurtured.

Agape love is the kind Paul was talking about in the Love Chapter. He begins the discussion on love by saying, "If I had the gift of speaking in other languages without learning them; if I could speak every language there is in all of heaven and earth but didn't love others, I would only be making a noise. If I had the gift of prophecy and knew all about what is going to happen in the future and knew everything about everything, but didn't love others, what good would it be? If I had the gift of faith so that I could speak to a mountain and make it move, I would still be ineffective without love. If I gave everything I had to poor people without giving them love, and if I were burned alive for preaching the gospel but it wasn't accompanied by love, there would be no value in it. No value. It would be worth nothing without love" (see 1 Cor. 13:1-3).

When the world talks about love it's talking about a tinsel kind of love—a love that's not lasting, based primarily upon the sensual and the physical, not real love.

Love and Sex Are Not the Same

In the book *Dating, Waiting and Choosing a Mate*, by H. Norman Wright and Marvin Inmon, is a chart that shows the difference between love and sex. The authors preface the chart by saying, "Often people associate sex with being intimate. But there is a difference. There are different types of intimacy. There is also a difference between sex and love. Some people say that they have loved another person when they have had sex with him. But that isn't necessarily true. Many people have sexual intercourse but love has nothing to do with what went on. Notice the differences between love and sex."[27]

LOVE...	SEX...
... is a process; you must go through it to understand what it is.	... is static; you have some idea of what it is like prior to going through it.
... is a learned operation; you must learn what to do through first having been loved and cared for by someone.	... is known naturally; you know instinctively what to do.
... requires constant attention.	... takes no effort.
... experiences slow growth—takes time to develop and evolve.	... is very fast—needs no time to develop.
... is deepened by creative thinking.	... is controlled mostly by feel—that is, responding to stimuli.

. . . is many small behavior changes that bring about good feelings.	. . . is one big feeling brought about by one big behavior.
. . . is an act of will with or without good feelings—sometimes "Don't feel like it."	. . . is an act of will—you feel like it.
. . . involves respect of the person to develop.	. . . does not require the respect of the person.
. . . is lots of warm laughter.	. . . is little or no laughter.
. . . requires knowing how to thoughtfully interact, to talk, to develop interesting conversations.	. . . requires little or no talking.
. . . develops in depth to sustain the relationship, involves much effort, where eventually real happiness is to be found.	. . . promises permanent relationship but never happens, can't sustain relationship, forever is an illusion.[28]

The problem as I see it is that adolescents, particularly girls, need to realize that sexual intimacy is not an indication of love. There will always be people in this world who will use and abuse you. It's hard to fathom a person who would put razor blades in Halloween apples so that little children would be hurt or who would encourage an incestual relationship or who delights in degrading the dignity of human life. But there are all kinds of people in the world, and some of them are out to hurt.

The solution is to determine who is good and who isn't, or who is good *for you* and who isn't. I worked with a young divorced woman several years ago. She had been through some rough times. Now that she was divorced she was seeking a new relationship. I said, "I know it's hard for a 27-year-old woman to meet men."

Connie replied, "Oh, no, it isn't. My roommate meets

guys all the time."

I replied, "Oh, gee, that's interesting. Tell me how, because I have a lot of divorced or widowed women coming here who are looking for ways to meet a man."

She answered, "It's really simple. She just goes to a bar and buys herself a drink. Pretty soon some man will buy her another drink, and they just sort of talk."

I pressed the point further to see what transpired. Connie's roommate would end up either at her apartment or his and, of course, have sex.

I looked at Connie and asked, "You mean to tell me that she can meet a guy, let him buy her a $1.75 drink, maybe even two or three or five, and then within a two-hour period she's in the sack with the guy?" She nodded yes. I said, "Connie, if that's what you call meeting people, hey, they're a dime a dozen. You can always find a guy who will use or abuse you." Nothing permanent will ever come out of this kind of relationship.

There's an amazing similarity between a 27-year-old divorcée and a 16-year-old adolescent. They are both vulnerable and very susceptible to being used. And they are both starving for love and affection from men. This is usually because they had a crummy relationship with the father or husband or both, so they go through life looking for some kind of permanent relationship with males, only to come up empty and dry.

Parents, tell your daughters that if their boyfriends want them to "prove" their love by going all the way, remember that the boys are not willing to prove their love by waiting until they are married. True love has to be developed. It can't be proven by the sex act. Tell your daughters not to let any guy use or abuse them for whatever reason.

Your daughter can find the kind of love that is lasting, satisfying and meaningful if she demands time to develop it. Not only will she do herself a favor, she will also do her boyfriend a favor by letting him know that she is too special to be used. Guys soon recognize who the special girls are, and special guys will seek them out as lifetime partners.

Someone once said that women give sex in order to be loved. I think there is a lot of truth to that statement. But a girl should ask herself, "Do I really feel loved when I am in the middle of intercourse? Do I feel cared for after it's finished, or do I feel used?" Almost all women tell me that the times when they feel loved are when they are caressed, treated with respect, and looked upon as special. I think a letter to Ann Landers said it best.

Dear Ann: In a recent column someone wrote about a husband who was unable to perform sexually after a prostate operation. A penile implant was suggested.

My husband has been impotent for three years (also prostate trouble) and he is only 59. We have a wonderful life together—in every way. The sexual aspect of our marriage is much more satisfying to me than it was with my first husband, a handsome and virile man who demanded sex seven nights a week and twice on Sunday. But he knew nothing about making love—for him it was purely a physical exercise, a highly impersonal act. There was never any caressing or words of endearment. He showed no interest in me beyond the fact that I was the vehicle for his bedroom acrobatics. Although he was very bright in other areas (actually an intellectual), his ignorance and insensitivity never failed to amaze me.

I do not miss sexual intercourse in the least. I am completely satisfied with tender caresses and loving kisses. I adore being held close. Falling asleep in the arms of my beloved is my idea of heaven.

Believe me, Ann, I wouldn't have that stud back for all the money in the world.—Had It Both Ways.

Dear Both Ways: I wish a copy of your letter could be attached to every marriage license issued in the Western world. Since it isn't possible, perhaps it might help to leave this column on the pillow of the man who needs to see it.

How strange that many males who consider themselves enlightened—even sophisticated—don't know the difference between having sex and making love.

When women write to me about this problem I encourage them to communicate their feelings. Some men need to be told what is pleasing. And some women need verbal guidance, too. A mutually satisfying sexual relationship is not a gift—it is an achievement. And well worth the effort.[29]

Chapter 6

"Where Have You Been?"
"Out!"
"What Did You Do?"
"Nothing!"

Adolescents are famous for wanting the best of both worlds. On one hand they say, "Get out of my life, leave me alone, give me space." On the other hand they say, "Hey, Mom and Dad, take care of me. Every time I get in a hassle or need a few extra bucks I want you to bail me out."

Adolescents live on emotions. One day they're sky high and the next they're valley low. Consequently, the emotional life of the teenager is usually topsy-turvy, not by design but by their very nature; and often they end up hurting those who are closest to them—their family members.

What's the best way for us as parents to handle these kids during their teenage years? The easiest way is to say, "If we just love them enough everything will work out okay." This couldn't be further from the truth. Love is not complete without discipline. "If you refuse to discipline your son, it proves you don't love him; for if you love him you will be prompt to punish him" (Prov. 13:24). Now *discipline* doesn't mean to punish only; discipline means to teach, to disciple, to show the way. Parents need to give guidelines, set limits, establish rules and enforce them.

Many parents, although they have head knowledge about the rules and regulations that are necessary at home, suffer from the good-parent complex. They have a difficult time trying to enforce the rules and regulations for fear the children might, in fact, reject their parents.

Guidelines are important because they communicate to our children that we care what happens to them. The kids may not always agree with our guidelines, but that's all right. They also need something to bounce off of, to resist if you will, because resistance is what builds strength. Regulations which teenagers resist will help keep them on a course that is instructive, not destructive, and will help them build the muscle they will need when they are on their own, making their own decisions. So children, for their own sakes, must be taught to respect and obey parental authority.

The first miracle Jesus performed was when He accompanied His mother to a wedding in the village of Cana in Galilee. During the wedding festivities the wine supply ran out "and Jesus' mother came to Him with the problem.

" 'I can't help you now,' he said. 'It isn't yet my time for miracles.' But his mother told the servants, 'Do whatever he tells you to.'

"Six stone waterpots were standing there; . . . perhaps twenty to thirty gallons each. Then Jesus told the servants to fill them to the brim with water. When this was done he said, 'Dip some out and take it to the master of ceremonies.' When the master of ceremonies tasted the water that was now wine, not knowing where it had come from (though, of course, the servants did), he called the bridegroom over. 'This is wonderful stuff!' he said.

'You're different from most. Usually a host uses the best wine first, and afterwards, when everyone is full and doesn't care, then he brings out the less expensive brands. But you have kept the best for last!' " (John 2:4-10).

This miracle, to me, demonstrates two principles. First, even the Son of God, Jesus Christ Himself, obeyed His mother. There are several other instances in God's Word where Jesus obeyed His earthly parents. Second, when Jesus did something He always did it first class. He turned the water into the *best* wine. I think that's an important point for us to ponder as Christians. We don't have to feel inferior to anyone. We also have the responsibility to strive for top quality in all we do because we are children of God. We're very special people.

This is the message we have to impart to our children: (1) they have to respect and obey us as parents; (2) they are special people, created by God to be His children; therefore, (3) they have a right to expect the best God has for them.

Okay, easy said. Now how do we go about setting up the guidelines that will impart these truths? Following are 20 tried-and-true steps you can take on a day-to-day basis with your children to keep open communication with them until they can stand on their own.

1. Don't Threaten

If you say something is going to happen by way of discipline, be sure it happens. Don't say anything unless you intend to follow through. There's nothing worse than telling a child or adolescent that if he does thus and thus you will react by doing thus and thus, unless you *do* react in that way. What you are doing when you don't follow through is teaching the child that Mom or Dad's word doesn't really mean a thing. For heaven's sake, or really for your child's sake, think before you threaten. If major decisions need to be made, sleep on them a night or two and talk about them with your spouse before the two of you approach your teenager to discuss it.

2. Watch Your Expectations

Many times parents unknowingly place unrealistic expectations on their children, especially their firstborn children. Standards need to be realistic. You can't impose super-high expectations for your children and maintain an encouraging situation. We live in a world that is perfectionistic-oriented. We are great at picking out flaws rather than the good in people. If parents join the world and also impose unrealistic expectations on their teenagers, they often push them to the brink.

Parents often impose extremely high standards on their children because one or both of *them* were firstborn or only children. Firstborns feel very comfortable with strict rules and regulations and high standards. But some children are not able to cope with unrealistic expectations placed upon them.

3. Accept Him Where He Is

It's tough to accept your own child where he is. We don't always have trouble accepting other people's children where they are, but we know how we want our children to be, how we want them to think and act. We don't have to agree with the way our children are, but we do have to communicate that we care for them. We have to accept our teenager where he is. Remember that our model, as Christians, is Jesus. Jesus always met people where they were. He meets us now where we are.

Most parents are extremely good at extinguishing their children's feelings while they are still very young. But if your child or teenager has feelings or opinions about anything which happen to conflict with yours, try to recognize that he has a right to his feelings, hear him out, accept him as he is, then go on from there. If he is immature in the way he thinks, your understanding him and accepting him anyhow will go a long way toward helping him sort out his feelings. However, he may never totally agree with his parents on everything.

4. Take Time to Listen

This ties in with accepting your child. If you want a relationship with your child, if you want to still be friends with your child when he becomes a man or she becomes a woman, take time to listen. Listening means that your entire energy is geared toward just trying to hear and feel what your child is trying to tell you. Don't be judgmental because you disagree, and don't spend your listening time preparing what you're going to say when he's finished. Really listen.

5. Respect His Choices

Another tough assignment for us as parents is to respect our children and their choices.

After all, we know what clothes look best on our children; we know what friends are best for our children; we know what activities our children should engage in—we know everything our children should do, say and be. Now why can't they just submit and let us live their lives? We know what's best.

There were some interesting studies done of elementary-age children who were allowed to eat anything they wanted in a school cafeteria during a month of testing. At the beginning of the month-long experiment the children, of course, pigged out on the desserts, sweets and all the goodies. But as the days marched by they began to swing back to a very traditional and well-balanced diet. Kids love to test us. They are going to selectively like things they know we don't just to see if we will love them even though we disagree with them. They want us to respect their choices. Much rebellion during the teen years comes about because kids want their choices—right or wrong—to be respected. Many parents, who had to learn to respect their children's choices, say that now that the kids are grown they have become more like their mother and father than their parents ever would have hoped or thought.

6. Ask for Forgiveness

Too many parents feel they should never have to ask for forgiveness from their child or teenager because they feel they are better. No way! We're all the same; we all fall short. I've seen what happens when parents go in a humble manner to their child and say, "Hey, forgive me." To admit that we were insensitive, cruel, mean, forgetful— whatever, to a teenager really makes us stand tall in our adolescent's eyes. When we can admit that we blew it, all kinds of avenues open up for our children to share with us.

7. Respect His Privacy

During the adolescent years, as emotions run high and new sexual feelings run rampant in an adolescent's body, your kids need you to step back and let them have their privacy. It's hard to handle the fact that your little boy or little girl doesn't want to crawl into your lap anymore, or go for a ride in the family car, or do much of anything with the family. You really get the feeling that the kid is only interested in having a bunk at the house and some food on the tale to keep him going so he can keep up with his busy social life, answer the phone constantly and attend to his duties at school. But he's building his independence while still under the shelter of your love and concern. Help him by respecting his privacy.

8. Share Your Feelings

If your adolescent asks you, tell him how you feel. One thing I am so thankful to God for is that my parents always told me how they felt about things. They told me clearly and succinctly and yet they let me make my decisions about things. To me that's a realistic way of sharing with a teenager. Share clearly how you feel.

That reminds me of the story of a country church that struggled for over a year to buy a new chandelier for the sanctuary. They had a promotional campaign and already had the approval of the committee in charge of church expenditures. But it had to go before the congregation, and for an item as costly as this, 100 percent of the congregation needed to approve it. The chairman of the church stood up and asked for the final vote. It was almost unanimous; one old farmer in the back row voted no. So the chairman called for a revote after a few more words of encouragement. Again the farmer voted no. Finally the chairman queried the old man as to why he was resisting buying the chandelier. The old fellow replied, "There's too many other things this church needs, like a light in the sanctuary."

Speak directly to your kids. Call it as you see it. Don't try to dazzle them.

9. Do the Unexpected

Doing the unexpected can be a very good way of communicating respect to children and teenagers and also of making them accountable for the choices they make. For example, suppose Mom and Dad have asked their teenage son and daughter to start dinner. Mom and Dad come home, perhaps after working all day, and find the dirty breakfast dishes still in the sink and nothing started for dinner. Where are the teenagers? Watching late afternoon television. What do we as parents usually do? Most of us go in, ranting and raving about how undependable those kids are, and stomp around the house creating ill feelings. Then to add fuel to the fire, Mom and Dad go into the kitchen, roll up their sleeves and proceed to clean up and prepare dinner, letting the children off the hook.

I contend that a good way to handle the situation might be for Mom and Dad to simply turn around and leave the house. Go out to dinner by themselves and make an evening of it. I would repeat that procedure until such time as the children did as they were told to do. Now, you say, that might be expensive and inconvenient. But isn't it a nice way to have dinner with your husband or wife without the teenagers around?

The point is, we need to hold children responsible for what we expect of them. That's our responsibility as parents. We can't beat them over the heads and make them do things, but neither can we play into their hands. So doing the unexpected sometimes can really be effective.

10. Talk About Potential Problems

It is really important to share with your children some of the pitfalls and challenges that lie before them. Again, here is an opportunity to share with them from your own life. Whenever we do that we open good avenues of communication. Talking to a 13- or 14-year-old about when he begins dating at 16 is, in my opinion, a good thing to do. Such communication gives your child time to prepare and will help him or her make rational decisions and be better prepared for many things that can happen. Also the teenager will be more receptive to you when you talk about problems before he has to meet them. The day before the first date is much too late.

11. Don't Act Like a Teenager

It's a temptation for many of us to feel that by not act-ing our age, we identify with our youngsters and make them feel comfortable with us. Actually the reverse is true. Kids who have parents that act, look and talk like teenagers tell me that they feel very self-conscious and embarrassed when their moms or dads try to be teenag-ers. Most adolescents want us as parents to act, look and talk like parents. That's our role. They have plenty of buddies; they need parents. There is a difference.

12. Give Him Choices; Let Him Fail

A tough assignment, especially if you were a firstborn or an only child, is to give your children choices and let them fail. Those of us who feel that we have to control sit-uations in other people find it particularly difficult to give our children choices. There's something anti-American about letting people fail. Yet think about the time when your life turned around, when you began to put things together. Did that experience come out of success or out of failure? If you're like most of us, the good, dramatic changes came out of failure.

Giving a teenager, for example, the choice of mowing the lawn or paying someone else to mow it for him is a good technique. It says, "Hey, you have a choice. Do you want the privilege of paying someone else to do it for you, or to do it yourself?" This method gets our teenagers a little closer to life's realities. As an adult who likes to drive a clean car, I have a choice: should I clean it myself or be lazy and pay four bucks at the carwash? See, life's training ground has to be similar to what real life is all about. There are real responsibilities in the world and kids have to learn how to handle them while they're still in the home. It's the safest place in the world to learn about the realities of life.

13. Don't Snowplow His School Road

Don't interfere in your child's or adolescent's school life to the point where you take away his incentive and sense of responsibility for his own education. What? Stay out of their school life when just last week the president of the PTA made a speech about parents and children working together to help expand the mind of today's youth? I'm telling you that when you get involved in a kid's school work and activities, 90 percent of the time that involvement is negative involvement. It's important that teenagers learn early in their childhood that their education is their own responsibility; it's no one else's; and they are going to be held accountable for what they do with the opportunity.

Actually, even kindergartners don't want their parents to be too obvious around their school. One mother I know was going on a field trip with her son's kindergarten class. The little boy said, "Please don't sit near me." Children want their school life separate from their home life.

This is not to say that parents should not give a child encouragement in his homework, or that they shouldn't see to it that he sets aside time to do his homework; but parents should resist the temptation to help him with it or do it for him or try in any way to make it easier for him.

Parents also ought to see to it that the schools encourage responsibility in their children. I recently worked with a family who literally had to beat on the high school principal's desk to get him to flunk their freshman son. All the boy's grades for the entire year were Ds and Fs. The kid wasn't learning according to the school's own report system. Yet the school authorities had the audacity to say they were going to promote him to the next grade because they thought it would be bad for him to stay back with the younger children.

Now how are we ever going to teach accountability and responsibility training to children when our system tells them that no matter what they do and how badly they fail, they'll pass anyway? "Don't worry, you'll still get to go through graduation—wear the funny cap and gown, sing a few songs and go to the party with the rest of the guys." Now, that's crazy!

14. Neither Show Him Off Nor Embarrass Him

Every family has at least one kid who's talented, clever, cute or outstanding in some way. Some people have a whole houseful of kids like that. But, please, spare the kids—and your friends; don't embarrass the kids by making them show off.

It's easy to fall into the trap of showing off your children. Sure you're proud of their accomplishments, whatever they are. But to ask your talented son or daughter to perform for your friends or relatives without first preparing them is putting them on the spot. You wouldn't like someone to put you on the spot that way. Why would you put your teenager on that same spot?

The other side of this is don't embarrass them. When your teenagers goof up, when they don't do the job they were supposed to have done, it's very tempting to browbeat them in front of their peers. How would you feel if someone did that to you? You wouldn't want to be ridiculed or laughed at before your peers by someone you love. So have the courtesy to wait until you're alone with your teenager; then if he needs chewing out, chew him out real good. A good chewing out never hurts. Tell him exactly how you feel about things.

15. Don't Be a Flaw-Picker

Traveling right along with embarrassing them is the problem of flaw-picking. Teens see enough flaws in themselves and they magnify their own faults. They don't need their parents pouncing on every little thing they do. Their self-concept is usually at an all-time low at adolescence. Many times it is low because their parents began to whittle away at it while they were very young; the first time your little one made his own bed did Mom come along behind him and remake it, showing him that he didn't do it right? Or when little Johnny helped to clean up the yard, did Dad show him how much he missed rather than how much he helped?

Children and adolescents need to be reminded, coaxed and encouraged to do what they should. They don't need to have someone constantly point out their weaknesses, failures and flaws.

16. Don't Spit in Their Soup

You know what "spit in their soup" is? That's when your daughter asks if she can go to some activity at school that night, and you reply, "Okay, go on along, honey, and have a good time. But you know how I am when you're out at night." See, the "spit in their soup" part is the little something you add at the end of the sentence that says, "Go ahead and go, but you won't have a good time because you know I'm going to be here at home worrying about you." Spitting in the soup is a sure way to create the guilties in your children and create a divisive relationship between you and your son or daughter.

Another thing we as parents do is dig up old bones. It's so easy to go back and remind a teenager about his spotty attendance at school or church, or pull some other little indiscretions out of the past which he has done or hasn't done. Digging up old bones is never instructive, it's usually destructive. Parents, think before you open your mouth.

17. Don't Talk in Volumes

Parents have a way of overdoing things. If your adolescent asks what time it is, tell him what time it is. Don't tell him how Big Ben was made and how it's maintained. Many of us just wait for an opening as innocent as "What time is it?" to bring down volumes of advice and instructions. If you talk in volumes your adolescent will tune you out immediately. Don't ever begin, "When I was your age . . ." It guarantees an immediate adolescent deafness.

18. Share Your Real Self

Be brave and share with your adolescent your real thoughts and feelings about yourself. You'll pave the way for honest, open communication between you. This is a difficult thing to do because many times we honestly don't want our children to know that we have another side to our lives. But who doesn't have some dark side in his past? Not one of us on this earth. We all have some skeletons in our closet that we're ashamed of and don't feel good about.

Now some of you are thinking, "Why parade that dirty linen in front of our own children?" Well, I think a lot of comfort and encouragement can be given to a child or adolescent when he sees that his parents are human— that they do make mistakes.

Try this exercise for what it's worth. Maybe after dinner some night have each person list on a piece of paper all the attributes and characteristics he or she wants others to think he or she has. Portray the image you project to others. Then on the other side list the qualities and weaknesses you know you have in your real selves. Now exchange papers—parents with kids. This exercise might generate some interesting discussion. As you explain why you said what you said about yourself, take the opportunity to tell some funny, amusing or even dumb stories about your childhood and adolescent years.

19. Don't Praise Your Adolescent

Okay, I realize that most of us grew up feeling that praise was important. In fact, I've see bumper stickers that say, "Look for the good and praise it." It sounds great, but I've found that praise can be a very defeating thing for your adolescent. How do you feel when someone praises you? I feel very uneasy. I feel that there's a hitch in it somewhere.

You say, "Yes, but how about the people who work for praise?" How about them? I know there are people who look for carrots every time they turn a corner. They constantly need someone stroking them. Fine, but what happens when there isn't someone around to stroke them constantly? What happens when your child or adolescent becomes an adult and can't find a substitute mother or dad to give them strokes? They fall apart. They don't handle things well when they're not praised or stroked. Have you ever talked to a pastor who had a church full of people who expected praise from the pulpit every time they did something for the church? Woe unto him the day he forgets to mention one of them!

What is a good substitute for praise? Encouragement is an excellent substitute for praise. The difference is subtle. For example, you come home and find that your son or daughter has surprised you by cleaning up the kitchen. In disbelief you yell for your 16-year-old Festus. "Festus, come here. Mom loves you. What a great job you did on this kitchen. Here's five dollars."

Can you predict what happens next? The very next day Festus is going to say, "Hey, Mom, where's my five dollars?"

"What five dollars?"

"The five dollars for today."

"Whatta you mean?"

"Well, yesterday you gave me five dollars for cleaning up. So where's my five dollars for today"? That's the kind of system you create if you go into a relationship with your adolescent based on praise.

The same situation: "Festus, come here. It's a joy to come home and see a clean, sparkling kitchen. So neat! I just want you to know I appreciate your effort so much." Give son a hug. What does that communicate? It communicates to him that Mom noticed what he did and she appreciates his effort. But notice that the emphasis is on his *effort* and not on the *job* he did.

The danger in praising a child or adolescent is that he might view himself as being loved or prized or appreciated because he did the dishes, and that isn't true. We love our adolescents regardless of whether or not they do extra work. Encouragement is far better than praise.

20. Don't Make Mountains Out of Molehills

We find it all too easy to be overly critical with adolescents. When iced tea is spilled at the dinner table your child doesn't need a tirade or a tantrum or a lecture. He just needs to clean it up. Many parents act like it's the beginning of World War III when their kids do one thing wrong.

What do you say when your son hands you his report card and he has three A's and one C? Do you get red in the face, grab your throat and scream, "Oh, no! A C! What's with this C?" It would be a lot better to say, "Three A's and a C! I'm really glad to see you enjoy learning. I'll bet you're proud of your effort." Chances are your teenager will fall right over on the floor out of sheer amazement. Think about that for a second. Three superior efforts and only one average. That's really a neat report card. But many of us feel compelled to go to the C and respond to it rather than to the three A's.

With an adolescent in the home there're going to be conflicts. When a hassle develops and you're feeling that uneasiness between yourself and your adolescent, approach the situation with a positive attitude. Pick a time and a place to discuss the problem where both of you are comfortable and can do so without interruption.

First, give your teenager the opportunity to tell his side of things. Begin by saying, "Robert, I'm very interested in what your feelings were and your reasons for throwing your younger brother into the creek." After your adolescent describes his feelings or reasons, take time to reflect back on what you hear. Give him a chance to clarify so that you understand exactly what he's trying to say.

Next, ask him to listen to your point of view. Again, remember while you are listening to him you aren't thinking of what you are going to say; you are just concentrating on listening. When you give your side, try to be as specific as you can about why you're bothered by the problem. Don't be general. If you're general you're going to leave room for misinterpretation and inaccuracy. Take time to discuss how you would have liked to see the problem handled if you could turn the clock back—which you can't. Then give your adolescent the opportunity to tell how he should have handled the problem.

Lastly, work towards a mutual solution to the problem. That's why we sat down and talked about the problem to begin with, so that we could come to an agreeable solution. There might have to be some compromise or some negotiation, but that's true of almost everything in life. If there is some doubt in your mind or your adolescent's mind as to what is expected, take the time to write out the agreement and sign it. Then if there's a need to go back and refer to it, everyone knows exactly what was expected.

I hope these guidelines are useful to you as you go through the teen years with your adolescent. Being a teenager or being a parent of a teenager is not a very easy task and it requires a great amount of determination and willingness to cooperate and much love and understanding to survive those adolescent years.

Chapter 7

Booze and Yooz

I recently worked with a young high school senior who had gone to a party at the university while visiting a girl friend. Of course she had a great need to be just like everybody else; so she walked around with a drink in her hand, sipping it. As many new drinkers do, she guzzled a bit too much too quickly and passed out at the party. Some gentlemen, who were obviously concerned for her welfare, thought enough of her to take her to their apartment. There they removed her clothing and, as best as we could determine, about 10 young men gang-raped this 17-year-old high school student.

Several hours later when she woke up all she had were some faint, frightening memories of what had transpired. What an ugly blemish and memory this young girl has to face. Why? Because she acted irresponsibly. She went along with the crowd and didn't use her head.

It's a sad commentary, but drinking totally permeates our society. When someone asks you out for a drink, that doesn't mean a Coke or a cup of coffee, does it? It means an alcoholic beverage. The leading drug problem we have in the United States is that of alcohol. We don't like to think of alcohol as a drug, but it is, and it is having a devastating effect on millions of lives each day.

Ninety-three percent of our high school students have tried alcohol and as many as six percent drink daily.[30] One research concluded that one-third of the country's high school students are problem drinkers, that is, they have gotten drunk more than six times in the past year.[31] Nearly one out of six young people in the tenth to twelfth grades call themselves "heavy drinkers."[32] The nation's single greatest killer of people between 16 and 24 is drunk-driving crashes. I'm sure you've heard the statistic that tells that in the past decade more than 250,000 Americans have died because of drunk drivers, which is more than four times the number of Americans killed during the 10 years of fighting in the Vietnam war.[33] These facts alone should be enough to encourage us parents to warn our children against the dangers of drinking alcohol. But there's more.

Doctors Raymond B. Johnson and William Lukash, in a booklet *Medical Complications of Alcohol Abuse*, say that "alcohol can be a catalyst for violence of all types. There are at least 100,000 alcohol related deaths in the United States each year: 50 percent of the homicides in the United States are alcohol related and 50 percent of all the felons in federal penitentiaries have alcohol related problems. One-third of the suicide victims in this country show significant alcohol intoxication."[34]

Claire Costales, author of *Alcoholism*, says that she became an alcoholic at 17. She began drinking in her own home—she was born and reared in Ireland—by sneaking drinks at parties in her own home or at parties in friends' homes which she attended with her family. Claire says that "if booze hadn't been presented to me as acceptable, helpful and glamorous, chances are I would not have chosen a career in alcoholism."[35]

This tells me that the burden of informing—modeling as well as teaching—our children about this great threat to their happiness, their health, and their very lives is on us, their parents. Remember that children and adolescents copy what is modeled for them, and the earliest modeling they have is in the home. If very young children see one or both parents socializing over liquor, offering it to their guests, they will of course assume that's the proper way to act.

At the same time, however, you are telling him that liquor is not good for him; he has to wait until he's 21 to drink (or 18, 19, or "older"). What does this do? It's like showing him a taste of good things to come, just as that vitally important symbol of adulthood, the car, is. So when that child becomes an adolescent and wants to impress his peers and be "grown up" he takes up social drinking. He hasn't been prepared in his home for the dynamite effect of alcohol (schools and churches make some feeble attempts at education), so the first time he or she drinks at a party it could end up disastrously.

Again I must remind you, begin talking about the danger of the drug alcohol to your children when they are very young. Reinforce the information all the time he is growing up. Keep the avenue of communication open between you so that he can share with you some of the stories and incidents he becomes aware of at school. Then pay attention to his life-style. In one chapter I urged you to respect your child's privacy, but we also are obligated to be very observant and attentive to his day-by-day activities.

Professionals who work with teenage problem drinkers suggest a number of areas where parents should be alert. Among them are: know if your teenagers are attending school each day or not; see if they are defensive when questioned about alcohol; be aware of behavioral changes such as extreme boredom, moodiness or exhaustion; know where they're going and with whom; be present if they have a party at your house; if they ever get into a situation where they have had too much to drink, and they call you to come pick them up, do so without recriminations.

If you should ever happen to find your teenager dead drunk, take care of his immediate needs, get him to bed. Then next day be direct and straightforward with him about what happened, while his head is still pounding from the night before.

I've used the generic "he" as I've described what to do with the teenage drinker, but alcohol abuse is a growing problem especially among women. According to Dr. Eleanor Hanna, Director of the Alcohol Clinic of Massachusetts General Hospital, "The cocktail party is replacing the tea party for many women. The so-called "two-martini lunch" is no myth. There is a total naiveté among many female patients who come to our clinic about their physiological inability to tolerate as much alcohol as a man," Dr. Hanna said.[36] Now here's one good reason why young women need to realize that there really are significant differences between men and women. As Dr. Hanna points out, men are apparently able to maintain a constant level of tolerance to alcohol, but the level women can tolerate varies greatly. This could be due to the menstrual cycle and the use of contraceptives. So drinking alcohol, as in most other areas, is a greater threat and danger to the female than it is to the male.

Maybe your adolescent, or someone else's son or daughter, is already having an alcohol problem. Perhaps you are thinking, "Oh, a few beers once in a while aren't going to hurt." But maybe your child is one who can't take a few beers once in a while and leave it alone. Claire

Costales points out in her book, *Alcoholism*, that "medical experts now believe that the tendency to alcoholism is hereditary; that there is a genetic differentiation between people who drink and become addicted and those who drink and do not."[37]

How can your teenager know if alcohol is a problem for him? He can't until it's almost too late and he becomes an alcoholic. Alcoholics Anonymous distributes a sheet prepared by Johns Hopkins University Hospital that is a self-test to determine if you are an alcoholic. Answer the following questions as honestly as you can.

1. Do you lose time from work (or school) due to drinking?

2. Is drinking making your home life unhappy?

3. Do you drink because you are shy with other people?

4. Is drinking affecting your reputation?

5. Have you ever felt remorse after drinking?

6. Have you gotten into financial difficulties as a result of drinking?

7. Do you turn to lower companions and an inferior environment when drinking?

8. Does your drinking make you careless of your family's welfare?

9. Has your ambition decreased since drinking?

10. Do you crave a drink at a definite time daily?

11. Do you want a drink the next morning?

12. Does drinking cause you to have difficulty in sleeping?

13. Has your efficiency decreased since drinking?

14. Is drinking jeopardizing your job or business (or school work)?

15. Do you drink to escape from worries or trouble?

16. Do you drink alone?

17. Have you ever had a complete loss of memory as

a result of drinking?

   18. Has your doctor ever treated you for drinking?

   19. Do you drink to build up your self-confidence?

   20. Have you ever been to a hospital or institution on account of drinking?

If you answer yes to any *one* of the questions, this is a definite warning that you may be an alcoholic. If you answered yes to any *two*, the chances are that you are an alcoholic! If you answered yes to *three* or more and want to stop drinking, call the local office of AA, or write to Alcoholics Anonymous, P. O. Box 459, Grand Central Station, New York, NY 10017.

Alcohol is the number one drug abuse in the United States. The number two abuse is tobacco and number three is marijuana. Following is more from Chuck's session. You remember we quoted him in another chapter.

"Hello. My name is Chuck and I thought I'd talk to you about some of the experiences I've had with drugs in the past. I'm 25 years old. I graduated from high school in 1975.

"I started getting high on drugs when I was a freshman in high school. I guess if you were to ask me why I started getting high I'd say it was probably because everybody was doing it, it was the thing to do and you weren't cool if you weren't doing it. Before I let peer pressure take over I used to enjoy telling people that I didn't get high or drink and didn't smoke cigarettes. I can still say truthfully that I've never smoked a whole cigarette—and don't guess I've taken five hits off a cigarette in my whole life. But with dope you weren't cool if you didn't participate.

"I have to admit the first coupl'a times I tried pot I didn't get too much out of it, but I kept on doing it and kept on doing it until it got to be where it was a fun thing to do. I'd go to parties and at first I'd really laugh a lot and it was just a good time. My friends and I would get giggly and all that stuff. The first couple of months it was a lot of fun—it was a cool thing to do. Instead of going to class we'd go out and catch a buzz. When we came back everybody saw we had red eyes and thought we were cool. So it was really neat to walk into class and let everybody know we were high. You know how everybody does, they walk up to you and talk so they blow their breath on you to let you know they were out getting high at lunch. That is pretty cool if you think about it.

"It wasn't till a couple of years later that I really started having adverse feelings about marijuana—I wasn't smart enough to see what it was doing to me but I could sure see what it was doing to my friends. It seemed that a lot of procrastination was happening in their lives. We'd get high in the morning and just kind of waste the day, just breeze through the whole day, not really accomplishing nothing, just lay there and watch TV, go play ball or do nothing. And you can't really live today tomorrow. I really feel strongly that you should accomplish something, whether it's learning something, bettering yourself physically or mentally or doing something. Inside I didn't feel good about just sitting around all day and not doing anything. And that was pretty synonymous with marijuana."

Chuck found out what many scientists and physicians have now proved, that marijuana creates a particular personality in its users. In some people the effects do not show up for several years; in others the personality impairment is almost immediate. These distinct traits are called "pot personality" symptoms: impaired short-term memory; emotional flatness; the dropout syndrome—out of sports, out of school, out of family; diminished willpower, concentration, attention span, ability to deal with abstract or complex problems, and tolerance for frustration; increased confusion in thinking, impaired judgment, hostility toward authority.[38]

More than four million children between the ages of 12 and 17 smoke marijuana regularly (these are 1979 statistics).[39] Denise Kandel, in one study, points out the tremendous power of peer pressure among adolescents. She said that those teenagers whose friends use illegal drugs are also more likely to use drugs.[40]

Of all the studies I have reviewed regarding the use of drugs by adolescents, one really hits the nail on the head. An article by Cynthia G. Tudor, David M. Petersen and Kirk W. Elifson tells that studies show that the *closer* the adolescent is to his or her parents, the *less likely* he or she will use drugs. The more *independent* the adolescent is from his parents, the *greater the likelihood* that he will use drugs.[41] That really says something, doesn't it?

If you're not taking the time to talk to your children about drugs, you'd better start. Drugs are as accessible to children and adolescents today as Hershey bars were available to us. Talk to your kids about drugs, about the values you want them to have. Share with them what God's Word says about defiling your body.

It's amazing to me the number of kids I see who seem to be determined to do themselves in. Several years ago it was my unfortunate task to call a mom and dad in the midwest and notify them that their son had overdosed. You see, he didn't pay much attention to what many professionals have tried to share, that the combination of booze and drugs is a deadly one. This young man had several beers and then popped some barbiturates. Early in the morning his roommate returned from his night on the town and noticed something very peculiar about this young man—his neck was blue. He was dead. A 19-year-old's life snuffed out because he was irresponsible.

I'd be willing to bet that his parents never took the time to talk with their son about the deadly nature of drugs.

Perhaps those parents didn't know where to begin or didn't have necessary information. There's no excuse for that today. Every community has all kinds of information about drug use. Ask your family doctor or the local community health service or the police department, or your public library. How do you begin to talk to your adolescent or child about drugs? First, let him know you really care about him as a person and would like to know how he feels about drug use. If teenagers see that their parents want to be close to them and really do love them, chances are they will open up, share their thoughts and be responsive to what their parents want to teach them. These are the kids who probably will not get involved with drugs.

I know it's scary. One thing I hear parents say continually is, "I worry about my kid and alcohol and driving the car, getting stoned, doing something that's totally irresponsible and out of character." Why do they do things that are irresponsible and totally out of character? The answer is, when they're stoned or so wasted they can't see straight, they are not able to respond as they would otherwise. When do many young girls experience first sex? When they're so stoned or smashed they can't see straight and can't remember the next day exactly what happened.

The reality of the eighties is that drugs are easily available. Your kids are going to have to make a choice whether or not they will use drugs. They are going to have to have the courage of their convictions to say, "No, I don't want to be like everyone else and just follow along." But they need your help.

Most of us have heard the story of Carol Burnett's life, how both her parents were alcoholics and the only stabilizing factor in her life was her grandmother, who really showed that she loved Carol.

Carrie, Carol's own daughter, started using drugs at age 13. By the time Carrie reached 14 Carol became aware of her intense drug problem and put her daughter in a hospital. In an interview she was asked if she blamed herself for her daughter's problem with drugs. Miss Burnett answered, "I did at first." She realized that her daughter was trying to cop out with the excuse that she took drugs because her mother was famous, and she too was thrust into the limelight and couldn't handle it. Carol said, "Tell me, who lives a normal life? I never did! I would rather my parents had been me and I had lived the kind of life my kids have than to have grown up as I did. Everybody is born with something they have to over-come." Then she said something I think is very signifi-cant. "It's their [the kids'] responsibility [to take charge of their own lives]. I had to deal with my parents—I don't blame them. I did what I could with myself. All kids have to do the same. . . . Everybody finds something to com-plain about—that's human nature. But we are all respon-sible for ourselves."[42]

How true! We are all responsible for ourselves. But parents are responsible for teaching their kids to be responsible.

If you've never taken time to talk to your children about booze, drugs and sex, perhaps today would be a good day to start. Some parents are uncomfortable talk-ing about these subjects with their kids. That's probably because their parents didn't talk to them. Here is a sug-gestion that might make it easier. Take your children, one at a time, away somewhere overnight or for a weekend—a combination fun and serious-talking time. While you're in the car driving to your weekend spot, when you can't look at each other eyeball to eyeball, begin to open up.

Talk turkey about the subjects you've been avoiding. There's something magic about frank discussions with others while you're out driving.

When younger children ask about sex or drugs or alcohol be candid with them. Take time to explain. Be relevant and not too wordy. Answer their questions seriously, frankly and without embarrassment. Don't put them down in any shape or form. You, the parent, have to be the most reliable source of information for your child.[43]

Chapter 8

God's Promise: You Are Something Special

This is an open letter to your adolescent.

Take a look around you. Don't you feel like most people are happier than you are? As we said earlier, adolescence is a time when things are exaggerated—when other people really do seem better off than you. That feeling is only natural due to the great amount of insecurity and uncertainness an adolescent has.

Think about Mom and Dad for a moment. It's hard to believe that at one time in their lives they also felt ugly, unwanted, rejected and insecure. If Mom and Dad have followed the suggestions I've made in this book, they have already shared with you about the real self-images and thoughts they had about themselves when they were growing up.

Of course, what's of prime importance to most teenagers are those very special relationships they form during high school days—not only with friends of the opposite sex, but friends of the same sex as well. Once your high school days are ended, however, as hard as it will be for you to believe now, the relationships will basically end. There will be a fracturing of the friends whom you now think will be your lifetime buddies. All of a sudden they'll vanish as they leave your community and go away to school, take jobs in various parts of the country or get married. The whole gang just sort of vanishes into thin air. You'll be lucky to see some of them at 10-year intervals at the old high school reunion.

Speaking of that 10-year high school reunion, it seems like a million years off. You really have a choice to make right now. How do you want to be seen at that high school reunion when you walk in there with your husband or wife? Do you want to meet previous lovers eyeball-to-eyeball? Or do you want to walk into a room where there are many people with whom you've had good times and without any skeletons in your closet? You don't have to look into anybody's eyes who will make you feel guilty or angry or hurt or any of those things—at least not as a direct result of sexual activity with them.

Your big advantage right now as a teenager is to realize that your virginity is yours, and there's nothing wrong with wanting to preserve yourself for marriage. The fact remains that once you fork it over, you can't retrieve it. You really have a choice to make right now. Do you want sex to be really special and sacred and something to look forward to? Or do you want to be like so many other kids your age who have too much too fast? Do you want to have sex be something dirty, nasty, a guilt-ridden experience for you in life?

I think you probably realize that the years ahead are going to mean many changes for you in your life. Right now you might judge a restaurant by whether or not it has video machines in the lobby. But 10 years from now you might judge a restaurant by their béarnaise sauce. All of us, whether we like to admit it or not, are going to do a lot of changing between high school and the first high school reunion. Take pride in the fact that you are special and different and not like anybody else. Claim that promise that Almighty God knows what's best for you and is going to lead you in the right paths throughout your life.

So as you approach adulthood and freedom and independence, I hope you do it with optimism and with a great deal of excitement, because there is an awful lot in life to enjoy and benefit from.

Of course many new experiences are exciting in the young person's life but there are a lot of scary ones too. Well, the good news is that at the end of this long dark tunnel called adolescence there is a world that can be what you want it to be. A world where you can be happy and have self-worth and an opportunity to accomplish some of the things you'd like to in life. Adolescence isn't forever, thank goodness. Things have to get better, don't they? They couldn't get worse. Can you believe that there will be a time in your life when pimples will become a thing of the past? That's reason enough to celebrate in itself.

I'd like to share with you what God's promises are for you. I share them for several reasons, but primarily because sometimes in our enthusiasm to go out and become something in life we forget the most important thing, and that is our relationship with God. In Matthew 28:20, God's Word states, "And be sure of this—that I am with you always, even to the end of the world." Now what does that say? It says that once you receive Christ in your life and become a born-again Christian, God is never going to leave you—even when you go down paths that aren't good for you; even when you make decisions that aren't good for you; even when you get yourself into hot water and trouble. It's not a qualified love, it's an unqualified love that says, "Hey, I love you and I'll be with you forever. All you've got to do is call on me and I'll help. I'll walk you through it." If you feel that you can go through life without other people, you're in big trouble; but, above all, if you think you can go through life without God, you're doomed. You're not going to make it.

Is it going to be hard for you to live the kind of life God wants you to live? Of course it is. Ask any Christian. Life is not a piece of cake. You're going to make mistakes, wrong choices and so forth. But the good news is that God is a loving God who forgives.

In 2 Corinthians 5:17 we find that God promises us that when we make Christ Lord of our lives we become brand new persons inside. We're not the same anymore, new life has begun. So what does that mean? That means that even though you aren't complete yet, a brand new you is in the making, a new spirit. Now comes the work on the rest of you.

Even after you become a Christian you will have to go back and ask for cleansing and renewing of your life— a little more repair and construction work. There are going to be temptations, always. You're not going to be able to overcome temptations every time. God's Word tells us that. But it also tells us in 2 Peter 2:9 that "the Lord can rescue you and me from the temptations that surround us" no matter how difficult a situation is. You can always look to the Lord for guidance. He'll be able to help you.

As you move along in life and as you seek direction, you might come to a point in time where you're sort of wallowing around and really don't feel the support and direction you need. Proverbs, which is filled with practical advice for each of us for everyday living, tells us in chapter 3, verse 6, "In everything you do, put God first, and he will direct you and crown your efforts with success." Think about that. Put God first in everything and He'll direct you and crown your efforts with success.

Want to be a successful person? Put God first. That's a lesson many of us have to learn over and over again. Because of human nature we have this tendency to say, "Well Lord, things are really good right now so why don't you just slide over and let me take over my life." The minute you do that and try to make it on your own, you'll usually end up flat on your face.

One way to develop closeness with God is to develop friendships with other believers. It's easy in our society to have two sets of friends—our Christian believer-friends and our non-Christian friends that we work with or play games with. Someone once said that "birds of a feather flock together." I think there's an awful lot of truth in that statement. In 1 Corinthians 15:33 Paul is talking about people you associate with. "Don't be fooled by those who say such things [things that are contrary to Christian teaching]. If you listen to them you will start acting like them."

If you really are concerned about a good reputation, then be selective about whom you run with and associate with. I realize there is an awful lot of pressure to be like everybody else. You know, 30 years ago if somebody smoked pot or engaged in sex rather casually, people were really surprised. Most people would be offended. The tragic thing today is that it's now reversed; if you don't go along with the group and smoke dope and be like everybody else, people have a hard time believing that you don't.

There're going to be temptations and you can't rely on Mom and Dad alone as you deal with these situations face-to-face, one-on-one. You're going to have to build your own strength and courage to say no to things you know aren't good for you. During those times when you really do feel insecure, remember what Philippians 4:13

tells us. "Hey, whatever it is, call on me and we'll get it done together." That's powerful stuff.

Sometimes when you choose the right path in life you're going to be persecuted and cut down for your stand as a Christian. But 1 Peter 4:14 tells us to be happy if we are insulted for being a Christian because that's when God steps in and gives us special help. If you're steadfast and faithful the Lord will bless your life not only on this earth but eternally.

As you face the everyday hassles of life, keep your nose in God's Word. Seek His advice and direction in your life by claiming the promises in God's Word. As you approach major decisions in your life, sleep on those decisions. Realize that there's a normal part of your life right now that seems to insist that everything has to be done immediately, but fight that tendency with cognitive thought. Decisions don't always have to be made immediately. Sleep on them and think about them. Talk about them with your best friend or your parents. In some cases your best friends might really be your parents; you might have the kind of relationship where you can talk about anything.

I hope this book has helped both you and your parents to be able to talk on an honest level, taking off the many masks we love to wear. As one 15-year-old girl said, "Boy, if my mom and dad knew what I did they'd die." They probably wouldn't die; they'd probably understand. They've probably been through some of the same trials and tribulations you're going through right now.

A final note: Take pride in the fact that you're crummy, that you're imperfect and need others in your life. I know you like to be cool as an adolescent and to act like you don't have a worry in the world. But those of us who work with adolescents daily know that there're plenty of worries in the world of the adolescent. You have to realize that if you try to shoulder all of those worries yourself, it's going to be a long, tough road. It might even be an impossible road. Share your thoughts and your burdens with your parents. Share your burdens with your heavenly Father. Ask and seek direction in your life.

God thinks you are very special. You're so special that He even knows the number of hairs on your head. It's hard to believe, but it's true because God said it. He says He'll meet your every need; what does that mean? Every sexual need? Of course He's going to meet those sexual needs. How? By bringing someone very special to you. If you seek God's direction in your life someone very special someday will enter your life. If you have the courage to say no to this world you heighten the probability of having that one special person come in and share the joys and pleasures and rewards of this life with you.

What price does God place on us? He gave His only Son to us that we might not die but have eternal life. One final thought: "Commit everything you do to the Lord. Then he will give you your heart's desires" (see Psalm 37:5,4). What more can you ask for?

May the rocky road of your adolescent years be tolerable, provide you with great learning experiences that will reinforce your understanding of God's great love for each of us.

You are something special. Very special. Don't ever put yourself in a position where you are used by someone or where you are using someone else. People are for loving, not for using.

"Kids and Other Creatures"

The following questions and answers are from Dr. Leman's column, "Kids and Other Creatures," which appears in several newspapers in various states in the United States.

Dear Dr. Leman: I discovered a pair of Designer Jeans in my 16-year-old daughter's drawer. The store tags were still attached, but when confronted with them she said, "a friend" gave them to her. The friend doesn't seem to have a name, and I'm convinced that she has stolen them. I want to handle this in the best possible manner, but can't seem to think straight, as I'm very upset. **Upset Mom.**

Dear Mom: I would call and explain the situation to the store manager. Tell the manager you're bringing your daughter and jeans back, and then have your daughter return them to the manager while you wait outside his office. If this is a one-time situation, having your daughter talk face-to-face with the manager might curtail any of this activity. If you start finding more items, counseling will be in order to find out why your daughter has developed this destructive need in her life.

Dear Dr. Leman: How can I tell if my teenagers are smoking pot? **Concerned Parents.**

Dear Parents: (1) Lack of interest in outside activities. (2) Lethargy (not to be confused with teenagers who like to sleep late). (3) Slipping of grades. (4) Non-caring attitude. (5) Social withdrawal from the family. (6) Dilated pupils. (7) A definable odor. Most teenagers will have some of these symptoms some of the time, and that doesn't indicate pot-smoking. You should definitely be suspicious if most of these symptoms are present most of the time.

Dear. Dr. Leman: I need your help. My parents read your column all the time. I'll be 16 in three weeks and I want to get my license. The problem is, my parents say I can't because my Eagle Scout project hasn't been completed. I think it's unfair to not let me get my license. They're really big on my being responsible. But the problem as I see it is that I am responsible. My grades are good, I'm planning on going to the university, and I've never given them any hassles. I don't drink and I don't "smoke up" either. My parents said they'd let me get my license if it's okay with you. **No-Wheels Michael.**

Dear No Wheels: I don't think your parents should let your get your license because I think it's alright, but because you really do sound responsible. Responsible teenagers ought to have the privilege of driving provided they are willing to share the expense of driving—insurance and gas. Getting your license on your sixteenth birthday is a very special day in your life. I hope this letter makes your day one to remember.

Dear Dr. Leman: Would you let your 15-year-old daughter date a boy almost 20? Our daughter asked us permission to go out with Rick. I suppose he's a nice boy, but we really don't want to encourage it at this point. What do you think? **Missie's Mom.**

Dear Missie's Mom: I know that I've told my own daughters that they can date at age 31. Of course, that's with their mother present. Fifteen is too young to date one-on-one, especially a guy who is almost five years her senior. I'm sure this won't be a popular decision with your 15-year-old. A lot of times parents must make unpopular decisions for the welfare of their children. I believe that children of all ages need and appreciate guidelines. Be thankful she asked permission. This, of itself, tells us that she values your opinion. Keep talking with her, keeping the lines of communication open.

Dear Dr. Leman: My husband calls the children degrading names like "stupid," "dummy" or "jerk." It hurts their feelings, so how can I stop this? **Sticks and Stones.**

Dear Stones: You can't control your husband's immature behavior. Suggest to your children that they explain to your husband how they feel when he exhibits his insecurity in name-calling. Constant name-calling destroys important relationships.

Dear Dr. Leman: I'm divorced but I'm willing to share the responsibility of raising my two children with my ex. However, he has been, on several occasions, quite intoxicated when he has shown up to take the children. I've refused to let them leave. The situation keeps getting worse. **Needs Help.**

Dear Needs Help: Under no circumstances let your children drive with anyone who has been drinking. When he is sober, explain to him that you are willing to let him visit but can't risk their lives when he is out of control. Lecturing him won't change his behavior until he sees a need to change himself. But you must remain firm in your decision.

Dear Dr. Leman: My 15-year-old daughter is smoking. Should I cut her allowance so she can't buy them, or tell her no smoking in the house? I smoke myself, but don't want my daughter to start this filthy habit. **Smokey.**

Dear Smokey: Allowance shouldn't be discontinued, but if she chooses to spend it all on cigarettes you should not supplement it for other supplies she might need. If you allow her to smoke in the house it would only convey to her that you approve this habit that you yourself indulge in. Better clean up your own act before you take on hers.

Dear Dr. Leman: My daughter has just started dating and she has made it very clear that she doesn't want us around when she is entertaining her boyfriend in our home. We would like to keep an eye on things, if you know what I mean. Should we allow her this freedom? **Concerned Mom and Dad.**

Dear Eyeful: Set the guidelines for dating right off the bat. You want to meet her date and spend a little time getting to know him. Tell her you will respect her need for privacy and will leave them alone in the living room after a brief conversation with him. You might want to take them some Pepsi and popcorn or something during the evening. As a parent you have the obligation to know your children's friends and don't need to feel guilty for caring about them.

Dear Dr. Leman: My 16-year-old son has become impossible to live with. He is talking back and his grades are slipping. Both my husband and I are very concerned. Whenever we try to talk to Harold he tells us to get off his case and get out of his life. Are we asking too much for a 16-year-old to keep his room clean and be part of the family? **Mom.**

Dear Mom: Teenagers need and desire privacy. This is part of holding them close when they are very young and letting them go as they enter the teenage years. When Harold says, "Get off my case," do just that. However, when he asks for money two hours later or the car keys the very next night, remind him that you are out of his life until a week from Saturday.

Dear Dr. Leman: My 13-year-old Susan worries me. She's really a very pretty girl, but recently she has begun to degrade herself in front of me. I don't know if she is losing her self-esteem, or if this is some kind of a stage that she is going through. How do I respond to comments such as, "I'm so ugly I wish I were dead."? **Susan's Mom.**

Dear Susan's Mom: According to Dr. James Dobson, Susan is entering the canyon of inferiority. She's probably setting you up; that is, she would like for you to respond to her with a reassuring remark about her appearance. When kids remark about themselves in a degrading manner, a parent would be wise to say, "I'm sorry to hear that you see yourself that way. I see you quite differently."

Dear Dr. Leman: I have a 16-year-old daughter who's very content with having everyone help her out. She's old enough to drive now, but has not made any move towards getting her permit. My friends all think I'm lucky not to have to worry about her driving, but I'm concerned about her lack of motivation. She depends upon friends or myself for rides and doesn't seem to have any problem getting places. I'm afraid she'll lose her friends if she doesn't start providing for her own transportation. Any suggestions as to what I can do to help motivate her? **Concerned Mom.**

Dear Mom: Your exact words are "everyone helps her out." It's way past time for a 16-year-old to stand on her own two feet and have an opportunity to act responsibly in as many situations as possible. It's time to stop babying her and being her personal chauffeur. Her lack of motivation is either from overprotectiveness, or at the other extreme, being defeated and not measuring up to your high expectations. Decide which it is and then you may have some insight into her inactiveness.

Dear Dr. Leman: We have a 13-year-old son who recently got into trouble with the law for vandalizing school property. I'm sure it's not his fault, but he has some friends who are always getting him into trouble. They must have put him up to it. Can we help him to see that it's time to find some new friends? **Troubled Mom and Dad.**

Dear Troubled: Let your son face the juvenile authorities on his own two feet. If your son is an innocent bystander he will undoubtedly find out that he needs a change in his friends. Resist the temptation to say anything about his friends. This is a lesson he must learn for himself.

Dear Dr. Leman: I'm 15 years old and want to find a part-time job. My parents would rather I stay at home and do the housework. (My mom works full time.) How can I change their minds? All my friends are getting jobs, and housekeeping just bores me to death. **Susie.**

Dear Susie: Mom and Dad probably have definite reasons why they don't want you working at 15. I personally believe that working at 15 is a privilege and should take place only after a teenager has demonstrated responsibility in the home and school environments. If you've succeeded in both fronts thus far, it's time to present your case to Mom and Dad. Emphasize your responsible nature.

Dear Dr. Leman: My dad never approves of the new clothes I buy. He always comes up with some comment like, "It's too tight." "It leaves nothing to the imagination," etc. I don't dress revealingly, but he seems to think I'm out for all I can get. How can I get him to see things my way? I can't wear a box to school and church, but he almost gives me no alternative. **Uptight.**

Dear Uptight: You don't say in your letter how old you are. I'll assume you're 16 or 17. Whatever Mom and Dad have done right in your preteen years is about to pay off (hopefully). You are old enough to dress yourself tastefully for all occasions. Talk to Dad about respecting your decisions. Each of us has to row our own canoe.

Dear Dr. Leman: My 16-year-old son has started bringing

his girl friend home from school every day. I like her and she seems to enjoy my cooking, but she's here until at least 9:00 every night. She's my son's first girl friend and I don't know if I should say something or keep the burners hot. **Future Mother-in-law.**

Dear Future Mom-in-law: I don't care how nice she is, I vote for the heave-ho. Soon your son's chores and school work will begin to show the effects of this continued entertainment. How about inviting your star boarder for dinner once a week and setting up some guidelines with your son?

Dear Dr. Leman: We were shocked to come home and find our 12-year-old daughter had gotten into the liquor cabinet. We were very distraught and don't know if we should lay low or discipline her firmly. **Need Smarts.**

Dear Smarter, Bud-wiser: More often children watch your actions and ignore your words. I assume you have alcohol in your home while conveying that abstinence is the only way to go. Snooky is hearing one message but copying what she is observing. You're confusing her.

Dear Dr. Leman: What will I do when my high school-age son won't get up in the morning for school? I have to leave the house at 7:25 in order to get to my job on time. I've actually dragged him out of bed and that doesn't work either. We then have a blow-up and I leave for work in tears. **Mom.**

Dear Mom: Why don't you buy your son an alarm clock? Don't say anything about his getting up or anything; go about your business. I bet you in a week he's having orange juice with you bright and early.

Dear Dr. Leman: We have a son, 14, who is *constantly* threatening us with running away. Every time we put our foot down he lets us have it real good. With all we've read about teenage runaways, it's frightening to even think about. Last night was a perfect example of what goes on in our home. At 8:30 on a school night he said he was going to go out and play some video games. We, of course, said no. He carried on so that his father finally relented. He came home at 10:45. We need some help. Any suggestions would be appreciated. **Frightened.**

Dear Frightened: Who's the organ grinder and who is the monkey? First of all, your son's threatening to take a hike is purposive behavior, that is, it's his way of controlling you. Teenagers allow us to parent them out of love and respect. You must gain your son's respect by following through on what you say. Don't give in to his power plays.

Dear Dr. Leman: We have a serious problem with our 13-year-old son. He has been stealing money from us. The confusing thing is, he really doesn't need the money. We're heartbroken to learn of his behavior. We are older parents and have tried to be good parents. We've given Buddy everything that he's wanted. In fact, he just celebrated his thirteenth birthday and pleaded for an Atari. So my husband surprised him (and me) with this expensive gift. During the same week he stole $125 from us. We have tried talking with Buddy about this, but he denies it completely. When we bring it up to him he becomes unruly, curses us and even throws things at us. This, as you can imagine, is very upsetting to us, especially at this time of year. Can you help us? **Buddy's Mom.**

Dear Buddy's Mom: I'm not one to recommend family therapy prematurely. However, in this case it's needed, and pronto. Perhaps one of the biggest problems that you are going to face is turning around what I call the "Disneyland Experience." That is, giving Buddy everything he has ever asked for. Why not, in lieu of Christmas presents this year, give him a letter, wrapped in a Christmas package, spelling out how much you love him. In fact, you love him enough, even in this late stage, to begin to discipline him. Children appreciate and want firm guidelines. You need to convince Buddy that you mean business. The letter in place of Christmas presents ought to get his attention.

Dear Dr. Leman: This is not exactly a marriage or family problem, but rather a personal problem. I am an 18-year-old, five-foot-five, 140-pound girl who has never had a boyfriend. I have my very own car, a job, a stereo, a weekly allowance and good grades. I'm very popular but I have never been allowed to have a boyfriend. Now I can, and a young man, aged 18, likes me and I like him. But how do I tell him I don't know how to kiss or anything else? **First Time Around.**

Dear First Time: You don't have to tell him anything about your inexperience. This is your first love, and since you weren't allowed to date earlier, you might be tempted to rush into things too quickly. I would suggest that in your dating this special young man in your life that you take it *real slow*. Get to know him well, spend much time talking, sharing ideas and having fun together. If you want to attract special young men, those that aren't like anyone else, then you must treat yourself as special.

Don't violate or compromise your values. Good luck, and enjoy your dating experiences. Someone said you have to kiss a lot of toads to meet a prince.

Dear Dr. Leman: Our 16-year-old daughter, Karen, dropped out of school two months ago. Since then, she sleeps till 11 or 12 noon, eats "garbage," and is getting fatter each day. She doesn't have a good self-image, and feels that everyone is against her. Even though she was failing in school, we think she has potential. We have tried everything, and nothing has worked to get her back to school. Any suggestions? **Karen's Mom and Dad.**

Dear Karen's Mom and Dad: It sounds like the education your daughter needs is one that teaches the realities of life. It's called a job. I wouldn't give her a dime for anything, in hopes that might provide her with some motivation to find work. Teenagers clearly understand three things: money, the car and privileges. In today's society there are many opportunities for teens like Karen who discover after a while that school isn't a bad idea.

Dear Dr. Leman: I have a 16-year-old son who does battle with me daily. We argue about anything and everything. I can truthfully say that we don't see eye-to-eye on anything. How can I get him to stop being so argumentative? **Robbie's Mom.**

Dear Robbie's Mom: Fighting is an act of *cooperation!* It takes two of you to fight. Notice that it takes each of you to know what to say to escalate the "battle" an octave higher. The next time an argument starts, go to your room, lock the door, and turn the music up loud. Refuse to fight.

   Sounds like you and Robbie need to work on respecting each other. Respecting each other does *not* necessarily mean agreeing with each other's opinions. Respect also means granting rights of privacy to each other.

A TEENAGER'S TEN COMMANDMENTS TO PARENTS

1. Please don't give me everything I say I want. Saying no shows me you care. I appreciate guidelines.
2. Don't treat me as a little kid. Even though you know what's "right," I need to discover some things for myself.
3. Respect my need for privacy. Often I need to be alone to sort things out and daydream.
4. Never say, "In my day . . ." That's an immediate turn off. Besides, the pressures and responsibilities of my world are more complicated.
5. I don't pick your friends or clothes, please don't criticize mine. We can disagree and still respect each other's choices.
6. Refrain from always rescuing me; I learn most from my mistakes. Hold me accountable for the decisions I make in life, it's the only way I'll learn to be responsible.
7. Be brave enough to share your disappointments, thoughts and feelings with me. I'm never too old to be told I'm loved.
8. Don't talk in volumes. I've had years of good instruction, now trust me with the wisdom you have shared.
9. I respect you when you ask me for forgiveness for a thoughtless deed on your part. It proves that neither of us is perfect.
10. Set a good example for me as God intended you to do; I pay more attention to your actions than your words.

For information regarding speaking engagements or seminars, write or call:

Dr. Kevin Leman
1161 N. El Dorado Place
Suite 213
Tucson, AZ 85715
(602) 886-9925

Notes

1. Ronald L. Koteskey, "Growing Up Too Late Too Soon," *Christianity Today*, March 13, 1981, p. 24.

2. James Dobson, *Preparing for Adolescence* (Santa Ana, CA: Vision House Publishers, 1978).

3. Donald Gerig, *Leadership in Crisis* (Ventura, CA: Regal Books, 1981), p. 41.

4. Koteskey, "Growing Up Too Late," p. 24.

5. Dobson, "Preparing for Adolescence."

6. Ray Willey, ed., *Working with Youth, A Handbook for the 80's* (Wheaton, IL: Scripture Press, 1982).

7. Carol Greenberg Felsenthal, "Teen Suicide—What to Do When a Friend Is in Trouble," *Seventeen*, April 1979, pp. 184,185.

8. Patrick C. McHenry, Carl L. Tishler, Karen L. Christman, "Adolescent Suicide and the Classroom Teacher," *The Education Digest*, September 1980), pp. 43-45.

9. "Did He Leave You with More Than a Memory?" *Mademoiselle*, August 1980, p. 106.

10. Midge Lasky Schildkraut, "The Startling New Facts About VD," *Good Housekeeping*, September 1979, pp. 227,228.

11. "Herpes: New VD in Town," *Ms.*, December 1980, p. 62.

12. *"Did He Leave You,"* p. 106.
13. *"Herpes: The New Sexual Leprosy," Time,* July 28, 1980, p. 76.
14. "Herpes: New VD in Town," p. 62.
15. Scott Kraft, "Unwed Mothers List Fears of Rushing into Marriage," *Santa Barbara News Press,* November 26, 1981, p. C1.
16. Alan Guttmacher Institute as quoted in *People,* May 4, 1981, pp. 56-60.
17. "Teenage Birth Control," *Society,* March/April 1979, p. 3.
18. Dick Pawelek, "Study Shows That Teens Lack Knowledge of Pregnancy Risk," *Senior Scholastic,* November 15, 1979, p. 22.
19. Nancy Evans, "Living Together—Who's Most Likely to Succeed or Fail?" *Glamour,* March 1979, p. 232.
20. Alan Guttmacher Institute, *People.*
21. Linda L. Hendrixson, "Pregnant Children: A Socio-Educational Challenge," *Phi Delta Kappan,* May 1979, pp. 663,666.
22. Katherine B. Davis, *Factors in the Sex Life of Twenty-Two Hundred Women* (New York: Arno Press, 1972).
23. "Teenage Birth Control," p. 3.
24. Alan Guttmacher Institute, *People.*
25. Ibid.
26. See Romans 8:38,39.
27. H. Norman Wright and Marvin Inmon, *Dating, Waiting and Choosing a Mate* (Eugene, OR: Harvest House Publishers, 1978), p. 145.
28. Ibid., p. 146.
29. Ann Landers, "Love and Sex Not the Same," © 1981 Field Newspaper Syndicate and the Tucson Citizen.
30. Lloyd D. Johnston, Jerald G. Bachman, Patrick M. O'Malley, *Student Drug Use in America 1975-1980* (Washington, D.C.: National Institute on Drug Abuse, 1981).
31. "A Head Start on Drinking," *America,* April 4, 1981, p. 270.
32. Clifford Berman, "Is *Your* Child a Secret Alcoholic?" *Good Housekeeping,* June 1981, pp. 215,216.
33. "Drunk Driving: A License to Kill," *Reader's Digest,* February 1982, p. 80.
34. Raymond B. Johnson and William Lukash, *Medical Complications of Alcohol Abuse,* Summary of 1973 AMA Washington Conference, p. 6.
35. Claire Costales, *Alcoholism/The Way Back to Reality* (Ventura, CA: Regal Books, 1980), p. 30.
36. Eleanor Hanna, *Massachusetts General Hospital News,* September 1981.
37. Ibid., p. 20.
38. Peggy Mann, "Marijuana Alert III: The Devastation of Personality," *Reader's Digest,* December 1981, p. 81.
39. Marrill Rogers Skrocki, "Marijuana—the Disturbing New Facts," *McCalls,* June 1979, p. 57.
40. Denise B. Kendel, "Homophili, Selection and Socialization in Adolescent Friendships," *American Journal of Sociology,* September 1978, p. 427.
41. Cynthia G. Tudor, David M. Petersen, and Kirk W. Elifson, "An Examination of the Relationship Between Peer and Parental Influences and Adolescent Drug Use," *Adolescence,* Winter 1980, p. 795.
42. Dotson Rader, "The Triumph of Carol Burnett," *Parade,* January 5, 1982, p. 7.
43. Lloyd V. Allen, Jr., *Drug Abuse* (Ventura, CA: Regal Books, 1981).